MW00965744

Words in Bloom

by Trisha-Ann Reed

DORRANCE
PUBLISHING CO
EST. 1920
PITTSBURGH, PENNSYLVANIA 15238

The contents of this work, including, but not limited to, the accuracy of events, people, and places depicted; opinions expressed; permission to use previously published materials included; and any advice given or actions advocated are solely the responsibility of the author, who assumes all liability for said work and indemnifies the publisher against any claims stemming from publication of the work.

All Rights Reserved

Copyright © 2021 by Trisha-Ann Reed

No part of this book may be reproduced or transmitted, downloaded, distributed, reverse engineered, or stored in or introduced into any information storage and retrieval system, in any form or by any means, including photocopying and recording, whether electronic or mechanical, now known or hereinafter invented without permission in writing from the publisher.

Dorrance Publishing Co
585 Alpha Drive
Pittsburgh, PA 15238
Visit our website at *www.dorrancebookstore.com*

ISBN: 978-1-6386-7269-2
eISBN: 978-1-6386-7620-1

Words in Bloom

The ultimate secret of life is the sure knowledge of death, for without it, man would not strive to leave his mark upon the earth.

author unknown

I started writing poetry in 1974;
much of this book was written by 1986,
but I did write poems in later years also.

My mark in this world is this book,
I dedicate to all the people
out there who have inspired me in one way
or another.

So, always remember,
when you help someone up a hill,
you get nearer to the top yourself.

The Many Moods of Me

I have many, many moods;
only some can be described.
Some moods, I show all the time,
and others, I wish to hide.

I have a mood of happiness,
where nothing can get me down.
I'll put you on your feet again
when I see that discouraging frown.

Also, I have a sensitive mood,
where my world seems to stand still.
I get this big hole inside of me,
which only he can fill.

On a day where nothing seems to go right,
I obtain a resentful mood.
I talk my foot into my mouth,
then I'm sorry that I was rude.

I think it is funny how moods just come and go,
sometimes so quickly, I don't even know.
I'd like for my bad moods to fade away with time,
and my good moods to be forever mine.

I have other moods that have no words.
For now, I will just let them be,
because they are such hopeless moods,
ones I hope you will never see.

Sing With Me

I want to sing you a song that you will remember,
one that will linger in your heart forever;
A song so beautiful showing the love you bring,
I want to make you feel like a king.

Then, once my song is done,
please say you'll sing along.
Sing with me, until eternity.

Waiting for you in my dreams each night,
just after I drift off to sleep,
with your devotion and tender ways,
I know your love is mine to keep.
Upon your face is an everlasting smile
that makes me believe we will make it through many miles.

So once my song is done,
come and sing along.
Sing with me, until eternity.

Once my story is told,
together we will grow old.
We have all we need to begin;
Together, we will make it till the end.

When my song is done,
say you'll sing along.
Sing with me, until eternity.

Seasons

To Angela

I wish for you the summer skies and all the beauty that passes us by,
then in the fall, I hope you see the graceful changing of the leaves.
When winter comes and snow begins to fall, it makes the trees look so tall,
then soon again, it will be spring, and the birds will continue to sing.
As the seasons change, I'm sure you will, too,
but no matter what, remember I love you.

Stars

May the stars in the sky be yours forever;
when you look up at them, forget me never.

Grandmas

Grandmas are nice, kind, and sweet;
they take a quick liking to folks they meet.
Grandmas tell jokes that are so funny,
and they always call you "Honey."
Grandmas can cook and make everything taste so good;
they don't make you eat all your vegies, like your mother would.
Grandmas pick out a special card for you on your birthday—
I would not have it any other way.
Grandmas spread joy throughout the Christmas season,
and all year round with no reason.
Grandmas are warm, friendly, and generous.
Ay grandma is super tremendous!
That is why I am writing this little rhyme,
to let everyone know that my Grandma is one of a kind.

The Way I Am

A day or so ago, you left.
Where did you go?
Do you care?
I need to know.
I think about it and wonder;
every day, my head is filled with thunder.
I just can't bare the pain no longer;
I wonder if I will ever be stronger...
That's the way I am
and will probably always be
until I can find a way
to set my heart free.
Once we shook hands
to be lovers till the end,
today, I don't even
seem to be your friend.
I could spin in circles
until this day is through,
but what good is it if when I stop,
I still do not see you?
That's the way I am
and will probably always be
until the waves come into shore
and drag me out to sea.
Now, you're many miles away
after you said you'd leave me never.
The lies you told me over again
lie deep in my soul forever.
I could dangle on a string
until my hands and face are blue,
but what good is it if when I stop,
I still do not see you?
That's the way I am
and will probably always be
until a storm comes around
and drags me out to sea.

Love and Summer

Being in love in the summer is a wonderful thing,
walking through the park and hearing the birds sing.
Seeing the sunshine and the bright kites fly
brings a very happy smile to my face;
I wish I could see a smile on the whole human race.
The warm weather makes me so happy, I want to shout
and tell the whole world what love is about
Walking hand in hand with the one you love and
seeing all things the way God does from above;
laying in the sand and catching a tan,
shooting the breeze with a handsome young man
going to the beach and taking a swim,
always to be right next to him.
That is what love and summers are for
and hoping they will be forever more.

If I Were a Bird

If only I were a bird, I'd fly high among the sky,
and I would chirp whenever a friend of mine passed by;
flying high up in the clouds or resting on an apple tree,
always to do just what I want, always to be free.
If I were an eagle, I'd fly high above our nation.
I'd never have to work—I'd be on permanent vacation.
If I could be a snow-white dove, I'd swim throughout the sea,
and everyone in the world would have their eyes on me.
If only I were a bird, I'd fly high up in the sky,
looking down on God's creation until the day I die.

Clouds

Soft, fluffy, pure white clouds,
making beautiful designs in the sky,
it's such an amazing scene to watch
as they go floating right on by.

In the Dark of Okinawa

The morning sun, so hot, so soft,
looks down on this gorgeous land.
When night comes and the world turns dark,
the sparkling stars take their stand.
A brilliant-colored eagle
just then flies overhead
and looks down on the tiger
who has not yet been fed.
They look as angry as the waters
crashing on the mountainside.
The tiger's eyes are weary;
the eagle shows so much pride.
The misty dark turns to dawn;
the purplish mountains are getting bright.
The eagle just flew overhead…
Looks like the tiger slept last night.

Just Being Me

Sometimes I thought I'd like to be a flower in a garden,
And when the snow began to fall, like ice, I would harden.
I think maybe it could be nice to be covered by a chunk of ice.
Through the winter, I would not worry
because the snow would melt in a hurry.
In the spring I'd be the happiest flower.
Every now and then, I'd get a rain shower,
but then again, on the other hand,
being me is just fabulously grand.

My Journey

I have a thousand miles to go before I find my dream;
each step I take is slower than the last, but faster than the first, it seems.
I find the ground at my feet all ragged, messed, and torn,
but I will find my way to you before my path is any more worn.
It's rougher than I imagined it would be, up and around another bend.
I can see so far ahead; I swear this road has no end!
I don't care how tough it gets—I'll find my way to you.
I'm not one to give up; I'll complete my journey through.
Just one look at you will be a treat. I'll see you standing over beyond
the road to greet me as I finish my last mile.
It will be so worth everything, just to once again see your smile.

Wishes

If I had a room full of wishes, wishes I know could come true,
I'd cherish them dearly until I could think clearly,
then I'd make all those wishes for you.

I'd wish for you the bright blue sky, and all the beauty that I have passed by.
I'll wish for you when I'm your wife, a long and happy, fun-filled life,
and when we have our first baby girl or boy,
I'll wish for you not to miss out on the joy.

If I had a box full of diamonds, diamonds too pretty to keep,
I'd hide them forever, forget them never,
and dream about them as I drift off to sleep

But I will never have a box full of diamonds
or a room full of wishes waiting to come true.
So, I'll make you a promise that no matter what,
I will forever stay here with you.

When You Left

I had the whole world in my hands until you broke my heart,
then you left, and I fell all apart.
I believed in everything we did; I was so confident.
Now, everything has changed, and my life is so different.

We'd take a walk late at night; you'd call me on the phone.
Now, I feel so empty, and I'm so all alone.

I had the whole world in my hands until I found you gone
Now, you'll find me crying, long after day is done.

I could wonder if you're ever coming back home,
and I could wonder when, but if I did and you didn't,
I'd only be hurt all over again.

Thrill

Lives greatest thrill is not knowing what tomorrow may bring
It's exciting: We get a new surprise each morning when we wake up.

Soybeans

Soybeans is a stupid name, and I hate them just the same.
Nixon says they are full of protein, and he eats them like a fiend;
then he says, "Have no fear," we will eat them for many a year.
Soybean food, and soybean milk; soybean shoes and soybean silk—
soybean this, and soybean that; soybean cars and soybean cats.
Nixon just loves all his soybeans; he even puts them in vending machines!
Who says Nixon is mean? He is just an overgrown soybean.

City Life

Life on the farm was getting kinda hazy,
I had to get out of there before I went crazy.
I had a lot of pity when I left for the city,
but I knew I could make it because I wasn't very lazy.
Well, I met some guy who owned a red limousine;
he had a lot of money, but he wasn't very keen.
He acted kinda cool, but he talked like a fool—
then I realized this just wasn't my scene.
Night clubs and late shows were very inviting;
some city guys were really quite exciting.
A one-night stand with a very handsome man
turned out to be not so enlightening.
My kind of jobs were not so easy to find,
but I found two and couldn't make up my mind.
One was easy; the other one, sleazy.
I felt like leaving it all behind.
Well, I found that city life just ain't for me…
I'm coming back home, and let this wild life be.
So don't be alarmed when I get back to the farm;
I guess milking cows is my cup of tea.

She

Goodbye to you—this time for good; I'm leaving you. I know I should.

All you ever did me was all wrong; now, we just don't get along.

I sure do hate to say goodbye; I know I can't help to cry.

I loved you so and always do; I know at first, you loved me, too,

then it was she who came along and broke up our little song.

You turned around and went with her. Now, you two are in love, I'm sure.

Our love song is mine now only; I sing it myself when I feel lonely:

Our sweet song of love and life and how I was to be your wife.

Now, it is she in your arms, and it is me you really harmed.

It is her in each of your dreams, and all you think about, it seems.

I'll wish the best for both of you in each and everything you'll do,

for it is her who'll be your wife. It will be her for the rest of your life.

Hole In My Heart

02/1995

When rainbows appear in the sky to brighten up a beautiful day,
someone steals the orange and blue and pushes the red out of the way.
Then, it's not a rainbow anymore—it's just a bunch of colors falling down;
and when they land in a field of dew, they never even make a sound.
When the snow falls to the earth and covers the streets in a blanket of white,
the sunshine comes and steals the show, then disappears into the night.
Then it doesn't shimmer and shine no more; it's all just dull and gray.
And when the morning comes around, I'm faced with another long, cold day.
When you came knocking at my heart's door, I opened it up and let love through:
I gave you all I had to give; I put my trust and faith in you.
When I believed your love was mine to hold, you stole it back and pushed me aside.
You shattered my soul beyond repair, and a part of me has forever died.

Keepsakes

04/1983

All that's left is an old photograph that has faded with the time,
and gently, I dream of you over music and some wine.
I remember the good times mostly, but some sad times, too,
and I remember your face when I'm with somebody new.
All that is left are the memories; times of you I'll cherish, I'll keep.
Softly, I dream of you when I take the time to sleep.
I remember the little things that always meant so much
and how the sparks would fly every time that we would touch.
But now all that is left is a photograph. I've drowned out all the sorrow,
and gently I think of you, my only keepsake for tomorrow.

My Own Memory Bouquet

Those two years I spent with you
are all wrapped up in a memory bouquet;
nothing could ever make me forget
the beautiful moments that came our way.

Amazing, like the pure red sun
setting in the country sidem
and I was stupid enough
to take it all in stride.

If I could go back in time,
I'd never ever let you go;
my love for you means so much
more than you'll ever know.

It's Not the Way

It's not the way you think of me;
it's not the way you care;
it's just the times that you forget me,
thinking that I was not there.
It's not the way that you loved me;
it's not the way that you showed it;
it's just the way that you don't tell me,
thinking I already know it.
It's not the way that you kiss me;
it's not the way you did before;
it's just the way that you changed it,
like you don't care anymore.
Could it be that you don't love me?
Could it be you won't let it show?
Could it be that you can't kiss me,
because our love can no longer grow?

My Search for You

I've searched my whole lifetime
for something I just can't find;
I've looked from New York to California,
and now I'm in a bind.

I'm out there looking for you;
a warm guy, big and strong.
I have not found you yet,
as far as I have gone.

All the while I'm searching,
I wonder just where you are…
Could you be around the next corner,
or are you somewhere far?

I have looked in Louisiana, and
Illinois, I just came from.
So, Tennessee and Kentucky:
look out—here I come!

Over the hills and through the valleys,
I wonder when this road will end.
Every time I think it has,
I find another bend.

I think I have looked every place,
but you, I have not found.
Before I go back home,
I'll take one last look around.

I walked around the corner
and into Delaware;
I could not believe my eyes
when I saw you standing there.

My search has finally ended;
my dream has come true.
I got just what I wanted,
now that I have you.

Thoughts of Freedom

When I woke up, I didn't notice the sun as it shone, sparkling on the bed.
I didn't hear the baby crying;
I was in my own small world, just thinking
the thoughts of freedom, dangling in my mind,
the thoughts of smiling people being so kind.
Then I closed my eyes and saw myself walking along the sandy shores;
for thousands of miles, all I could see was ocean and sand.
I felt so free.

Then you tapped me on the shoulder.
As I turned my head to look at you, you kissed me
Then I noticed it was spring;
the sun was shining in the window.
I heard the baby crying,
Then I realized I'd rather be with you
than ever to be free—
because I love you, and I know that you love me.

TF

If the sun doesn't rise in the morning,
don't bother knocking at my door.
If the sun doesn't want to shine,
just leave me sleep forever more.

If the rain comes tumbling down
and splashes at my feet,
you'll only find me in bed again
until the sun dries the streets.

If the flowers don't start to bloom
early in the spring,
I'll sit alone in my garden
and wish that I had wings.

So I could fly away to paradise,
and stay there till the end.
So if the sun don't wish to shine,
you'll only find me in bed again.

The Last One

I cannot write no more poems for you;
I've used up all the words.
There are no more that I can think of,
only ones you've already heard.

They are the same words over again;
the only ones I knew
that could describe the exact
way I felt for you.

So, therefore, there is nothing more
I can tell you that you do not already know.
So, if ever I do see you around,
maybe I'll stop to say, "Hello."

Without You

Being without you is like a bird without a wing
who has no reason to sing.

Being without you is like a dog without a bone;
he feels so all alone.

Being without you is like music with no words,
and never being heard.

Being without you is like a church without a steeple,
and inside, there are no people.

Someone Like You
06/1978

The sun was burning hot on my face;
The rain had no place to fall.
Then someone like you came along…
Once again, I'm standing tall.

My voice echoed through the hills;
reflections of daisies were in my eyes.
Peace could be heard in the valley below;
someone like you was at my side.

The grass that I was sitting on
felt hot as a winter's fire,
but that didn't really matter at all
because someone like you was at my side.

Dreams

06/1978

When the ships go sailing out to sea,
I dream that I go, too.
When they return to dock for the night,
I run home to tell you.
I tell you of the day I had,
with my eyes all full of glow;
a journey to a little island,
where such peaceful waters flow.
I saw dark caves and monkeys;
palm trees were everywhere.
Tomorrow, when the ships go out,
I'd like to take you there.
This big ship seems so small and lost
while we are out at sea,
but my adventures are so beautiful—
they all let me be me.
When the ships go sailing out to sea,
I dream that I go, too,
but that's all they are, is dreams,
that I run home to tell you.

Call Me Love

We watched the clouds change view above;
I turned to you, you called me love.
Now, I know how much you care—
Wherever I look, you are there.
The song you sang me was beautiful;
"*Love*," now is my name
I'm sure that in ten thousand years,
we will still feel the same.
Bunches of wild flowers
remind me much of you
till I fall off to sleep,
only to dream of you.
We lay in fields of clover
forever, and then a day,
you caress me in the sunlight
and vow never to go away.
I remember now;
you whispered in my ear once.
I'm sure that's who it was,
and that was the first time
ever you called me "*Love*."

Someone New
07/1978

I'm a rock on the bottom of the ocean floor,
sitting in the dark alone, and how do you feel
now that you've found someone new of your own?
Now, it's time to put the pain on paper,
so the world can see how you've done me wrong.
You took away my sanity, my wine, my dreams, my song—
I'm a tiny shell in the sand; to you, I am unknown.
How often do you think of me,
now that you've found someone new of your own?
I'm putting all this hurt on paper, so the world can see how you really are.
The only way you will remember me, is if I leave a scar.
I'm a pebble on a mountain of rock,
sitting here all alone, and how do you feel
now that you've found someone of your own?

Escape From Memory

06/1979

Where can I go where my memories will never find me
to be lost and alone, running anywhere but home?
Do memories always catch up? Do they stay forever in my mind?
I've got to get away to the highest mountain I can climb.
The memories of the past will not be able to find me there;
memories can't climb mountains, but can they travel through the air?
I've got to get away to the largest ocean in a boat;
memories cannot swim, but on water… Can they float?
I've got to get away to the deepest forest there is around;
there has to be a place where I am never to be found
by my memories, all the memories of the past—
how long can they chase me? How long can it last?
Where can I go? I've got to get away,
where my memories won't catch up.
Get them out of my life today.
I'd like to bury them under a stone,
then I can move on to my future,
and the memories would be unknown.
But…
Are they really gone? Or are they still with me?
I guess my memories will never let me be.
I've got to get away to the highest mountain I can climb.

Reflections

11/1979

Tomorrows will never be the same now that you are gone;
yesterday is just a fantasy that has set down with the sun.
I cannot put the past behind me yet; it causes too much pain.
Somehow, I know the reflections I see can never be the same.
The winter that lies ahead of me will surely be long and cold.
I never stop to catch my breath or let my thoughts be told.
The snow and ice will melt, I'm sure, and dissolve into spring,
but I'm still living in the past; those times mean everything.
Summer will be hot yet pretty, and I'll wonder where you are;
but you have a life with someone else you think of as your shining star.
When autumn comes around again, I'll still be living in my past.
All these feelings I hold for you are just strong enough to last.
Years go by and melt away, but my tomorrows will never be the same;
I'll live my future in the past until I'm strong enough to play life's game.

Forever

06/1978

I want to hold you in my arms; I want to hold you until the end;
I want to kiss you in the morning, time and time and time again.
You know that when I smile, it has to be for you,
and when I laugh out loud, it's because you like me, too.
I want to love you in the daytime, keep you by my side at night.
I want to love with you whenever, so we are always feeling right.
I'll try to keep you happy, so you're never feeling blue;
that is why I'm always smiling—I do it all for you.
I want to hold you in my arms, just hold you till the very end.
I'll kiss you every morning, time and time and time again.

I Don't Believe Love Is Forever

07/1978

You say that you need me, but it is only now and then,
so you go on to others, time and time again.
Just when I get close to you, I fill up with fears
because something always happens that leaves me in tears.
When things just don't work out, it is best to say good-bye,
save the memories of happy times to remember when you want to cry.
I don't believe that love is forever; I've never seen it happen that way.
So now, as I leave here, remember me and why I could not stay.
I can't help how I feel, but this is the way it has to be
until the tide comes into shore and drags me out to sea.

Love Again
07/1978

You have helped me to see things that I have never seen before;
you have taught me to hears things. Now, I want to hear more.
You showed me how to love again; you have turned my life around.
You've helped me through the long, dark days—I like what I have found.
Your kisses are so soft and sweet; your touch, one of a kind.
Your love is always gentle, and isn't so hard to find.
You showed me how to live again; you put my feet back on the ground.
You put the smile back on my face; I'm liking what I've found.
You make me feel so beautiful; it's you I'm always thinking of.
I want to say it one more time: You're the one I will always love.

Learning to Fly on My Own Wings
10/1978

I'm learning to fly on my own wings now,
and above it all,
sometimes very painfully—I may take another fall.

I'm learning to fly on my own wings now;
so much I've yet to learn.
I can look back into the times
that I have wasted and burned.

You won't see me walking the streets,
looking for a place to go;
and you won't catch me late at night
putting on a side show.

I'm learning to grow, and I won't let
another chance just pass me by.
I'm beginning to see eternity
way beyond the sky.

Mostly, I'm learning to fly on my own wings now:
slowly,
subtly,
and sometimes painfully.

True Love

02/1980

So many times, alone at night, I lie awake and wonder
how you and I came to be; my soul is like the thunder.
I walk inside this silent house, talking to myself out loud,
wondering why you chose me of all the girls in the crowd.
Now, we share a beautiful love, unique, so unlike anything else.
I feel your pain when you're sad; I feel your heart as it melts.
I feel your sorrows and your joys; I can see me through your eyes.
The vows we took will last forever. True love never dies.
I feel your emotions; we are so close, you're a part of me—
nothing can pull us apart. You and I are meant to be.
I sit and listen to the music, love songs written for you and I;
what we share will be forever. True love will never die.

I Stay, but There You Go

02/1980

I look, but I don't see; I hear, though no one talked.

I reached, but didn't touch nothing; I ran, but should've walked.

I climb, get closer to the top; I burn, but there is no fire.

I fell, but that's all right—I love, to find desire.

I daydream, almost all the time; I sleep, but not too much.

I cry, but there are no tears. I wish for a magic touch.

You came, but didn't stay; you kiss, but are too rough.

You try, till I say no; you leave. That was enough.

You turn, do you get dizzy? You lose, yet still go strong.

You run; you're in a hurry. You want, but don't belong.

You climb, get closer to the bottom; you look, yet never see.

You hear, only what you want; you ran, but not to me.

When You Called Me Love

02/1979

Are there words for me to say that would make you understand
what I am going through?
It's hard living so far away while I'm trying to remember just
how much I love you.
I remember how you would smile at me, but I don't recall the glow
in your eyes.
Every time I remember your laughter, I go numb and start to cry.
I can still remember the feeling I'd get when you would hold me close,
but forgetting the feel of your tender kisses is what hurts me the most.
I know you won't be gone a lifetime, but it sure does seem that way.
Every time the stars come out, I want you here to stay.
I remember the night we met, I was traveling through the west;
the times I spent with you were of the very best.
Then I had to leave, and I am here so all alone.
I just wish that you were with me; I hate being on my own.
I remember how we used to talk, but I don't remember what of.
I will never forget the first time when you called me *"Love."*

Sing

04/1979

You said that I would never make it; you said I'd never be a star.
So, you must have been quite surprised when I made it this far.
I sing my songs to those who listen, and I sing them right out loud;
and every town I go to play, I draw an even bigger crowd.
Sometimes, while I wait to go on stage, I think about the fortune, the fame,
which really doesn't even matter—the crowd goes home happily.
And that's the only reason why I came.
I write the words of love myself, just what these people want to hear,
and when my songs have been sung, the crowds will stand up to cheer.
Do you want to hear a love song? My band and I are here to play.
As long as I make this nation so happy, I will sing forever and a day.

Until I Find You There

04/1978

I live in a fantasy world where people will stop and stare;
I have only dreams to keep me going because no one really cares.
Whenever I get lonely, my imagination sets in.
I pretend I am a gentle cat or a race horse out to win.
I pretend I am an actress, and I live in Hollywood.
Or, I dream I am an inventor, who just invented something good.
Sometimes, I pretend I'm a country singer on my way to Nashville,
or maybe I'm a butterfly, or a statue large and still.
I pretend I'm the person in that portrait, looking like someone you once knew;
or I imagine that I am an angel, and my job is to keep an eye on you.
I live in a world of fantasy, but no one really cares.
My imagination will keep me going until I reach out and find you there.

A Gift for Jesus

05/1979

If I'd been here when Jesus was born,
I would've followed the star that guided the way.
I would've come with the three Wise Men
to celebrate this wonderful day.
His mother must have been so proud
when little baby Jesus was born;
all the animals gathered around
to keep Him safe and warm.
The three Wise Men brought gifts
of frankincense, myrrh, and gold,
but I'd have given Jesus
a gift He could never hold:
I would've given him a song just as beautiful as He.
A song of hope, love, and joy
would be the gift to Him from me.
Since I was not yet here when Jesus was born,
I fix a manger like the one where He lay
then I sing a song for Him
each and every Christmas day.

To My Friend, a Drug Addict

All alone by my phone,
waiting for you to call;
an hour passes very slowly,
then I start to climb the wall.
Baby, you drive me crazy;
I think your head is hazy.
That was all a year ago.
Now, you've learned a lesson;
you were fifteen steps up in the sky,
on your way to Heaven.
I tried to give you a helping hand;
I tried real hard to understand.
I tried for you.
Now, it's your turn;
you can wither, waste, and burn.
Don't you knock upon my door
to ask if I can help some more.
When your head is in the clouds,
I could scream right out loud.
First, you straighten up your act
and learn what life is for.
When your mind is clear again,
feel free to knock upon my door.

Easy Feeling

Looking into the clear blue waters, I get this easy feeling.
You can never tell my heart has been broken;
the beauty of the country side has got me healing.
The way the clouds drift overhead, it puts my mind at ease.
I never thought it could be this way;
it fills me up with peace.

Games of Love

Someone, take my hand; please help me understand.
Love is a rough game to be caught up in—
no one loses, and no one wins.
It's a game of pride, when someone is at your side;
It's a game of hurt and can make you feel like dirt.
All the same, love shouldn't be a game.
To me, love is very real. I like the way it makes me feel.
Love is something you cannot learn,
and you should be loved in return.
With some help from God above,
He has showed us all about love.
Now and then, I still may need someone to take my hand
because there are so many things I still don't understand.

About You

Your name crashes through my head
and whirls like a tornado in my mind;
it's you I'm always thinking of.
It makes me feel so very fine.
Your warmth burns deep inside me
and keeps me warm on a winter's day.
It may be zero degrees outside,
but your love keeps me warm like the sun's ray.
Your tenderness sweeps me off my feet
and makes me feel I'm floating on air;
there's no need to say you love me.
I feel it in the way you care.
Your kindness melts deep inside me;
it shows all over my face.
I feel it like a rocket ship
that just launched into space.
Your beauty comes and takes over my soul;
it makes my heart stand still,
then collides like a merry-go-round
that just rolled down a hill.
Now, I'm at a loss for words;
I have nothing else to say.
I've described you as best I could,
in every different imagined way.

Tinted Glass

11/1979

The pain stabbed me hard; like a knife, it left a scar.
I try to catch my breath as I look out through the tinted
glass in my car.
Your words melted like ice and left me speechless and alone,
and through the tinted glass, I watched you head for home.
I poured my glass to the very top with the very best wine.
Driving into the night, through the tinted glass, I could see
just fine.
Who is that hanging on so tight, walking by your side?
Is she another, unlike me, just out to get an easy ride?
The pain blasted right through me, like a bullet free and fast,
and I know I'll never see you again as I look out through
the tinted glass.

Tears of Gold

11/1979

Well, I'm not a fortune teller, and I don't wear black lace;
I'm not a lady of the evening with gobs of make-up on my face.
I'm just another person who has fallen hard for you;
I'm just another fool who cried the whole night through.
I know just what you wanted from me, and I'm not about to give it.
You've got too many others at your side, so take your time and live it.
You know, I'm not a circus clown, and I'm not a superstar;
also, I am not blind or deaf, so I can see how you really are.
I am not just another person who has to let her story be told:
I'm a treasure that no one has found, and I cry tears of gold.

Dancing as Fast as I Can

11/1979

At this time next year, I'll be a thousand miles away,
dancing as fast as I can, living for night, forgetting the day.
My clothes are made of tinsel; men long to take my hand.
The sun is coming up again… Doesn't anyone understand?
Running home to an empty house, sound asleep at last,
in bed, I lie alone once more, dreaming of the past.
I remember how you walked out on me; never again will I feel that pain.
I'll be dancing as fast as I can, living my life in the pouring rain.
At this time next year, I'll be someone you never really knew.
Some people say I'm as hard as rock, but that's the description I gave to you.
My life is in this cluttered room, a thousand miles away.
I'm dancing as fast as I can now, living for night, forgetting the day.

Silent Morning

12/1979

I never thought I'd see you again, but there you were once more;
I opened my mouth, but the words were stuck when you walked through the door.
I wanted to say how much I missed you; you're even better than a fantasy.
But the words melted in my mouth when you turned around and looked at me.
I wanted for you to touch me again, the way you did before;
I wanted you to kiss me again, and hold me close once more.
I don't think that would be enough; it never is when you're in love.
Now time is closing in on me—take me back to the way it was.
I never thought I'd see you again; you took me by surprise.
I opened my mouth, but the words got stuck when you looked into my eyes.

Just Once More

12/1979

In the coldness of the snowfall, driving home, I passed your door.
I know, deep in my heart, all is lost what we had before.
The reflection in your eyes and the sunshine of your smile
made me realize that we could only last a little while.
I was just too young for you; you said my spirit was much too free;
all the time we shared together brought the good things out in me.
Now, sometimes, late at night, I dream of good things we once shared,
I want to reach out and touch you, but you're no longer there.
I'll always have a place for you in the corners of my mind,
even though the feelings are lost, and the love got left behind.
In the chilly winter snowfall, driving home, I pass your door;
and I really should've stopped to kiss you, just once more.
Just once more.

Love Hurts

12/1979

Even after you've hurt me so much, I'm still in love with you;
You're always on my mind, no matter what you do.
I know I won't see you again; you walked away for good.
I don't think I can ever forget you, even if maybe I should.
I carry hopes and a dream with me where I go
of maybe seeing you again, the you I'd like to know.
If I didn't have these dreams of maybe seeing you again one day,
the pain and sorrow would settle in, and the hurt would never go away.
I'm still so in love with you; that's what I'm living for.
And every time I dream of you, I need to have that dream once more.
Some people say I'm crazy, but I don't really care
as long as I have my dreams of one day finding you there.

Time
07/1979

I wish today could last forever;
I do not want more time to pass.
Things around me are growing old;
I want this moment now to last.
Memories are not good enough,
because they never come again
And I have had so many good ones,
it's a crying shame they had to end.
Why doesn't life go on and on?
No one would hurt, and no one would cry.
We never have enough time to spend
with those we love before they die.
Why does life end with death?
Why don't we have a choice?
Why doesn't God hear my wish?
Why doesn't He hear my voice?
I want more time than life can give me;
that is all I'll ever ask for.
And when my time is running short,
I'll stop and ask for more.
I want all the time there is
from here to eternity,
and if that's not asking for too much,
then come and share it with me.
Why are days so short in hours?
Why do the years slip by so fast?
Life around me is growing old;
I wish this moment now could last.
Why won't someone come by and say
that time will leave me never?
Then we could go on and on,
to eternity to live forever.

The Owner

01/1980

Caught up in a web of men, a web of one-night stands,
until the owner came along and took me by the hand;
owner of time that isn't mine, owner of things, people, and a place,
owner of what he wants to have, the owner of this innocent face.
The owner was caught in a web of lies, and he dragged me right along;
never again to see the surface or the place where I belong.
There is no way I can fit in now; I am just like him.
Only he has gone on back home. Some things, I just can't win.
Now, that it is over and these scars will never heal,
I'm being hung from the sky; I cannot touch or feel.
The scars the owner gave me can never be fixed or mend,
but I do not even care anymore; the owner will never be back this way again.

Love

01/1980

I can't describe love now, but I never really could.

I think it is supposed to be happy; I think it is supposed to be good.

If love is all joy and bliss, then why do I want to cry?

If love is sharing dreams, then why have my dreams died?

If love is taking the good time along with all the bad,

then I do I feel so hurt? Why do I feel so sad?

If love is so confusing, then true love, I'll never know.

And if that's the way it is, then why do I want you so?

Through the Villa

01/1980

I run through the rain to see if the sun really does shine;
I run down snowy streets and wonder if you'll ever be mine.
I have no time to stop; I have no place to fall.
I have no hope to dream on; I no longer am standing tall.
I don't know where I'm running to, or what I'm running from,
but I know where I'd like to be when this day is finally done.
I'd like to be in your arms, lost within your smiling face.
All the times we've shared together is something no one can erase.
Those times will stay with me forever; I cherish them more every day,
and I would like to live tomorrow in that very same way.
But you won't be back here again; there is somewhere else you'd rather be.
And if you're not here tomorrow, then how can I be me?

Fools
01/1980

I really didn't want to see you anymore;
I just wanted to forget
all the times you hurt me,
the pain I'm feeling, and yet,
I went to see you anyway.
There you stood, so handsome, so tall;
all I needed was just one look.
And I knew I wanted to remember it all.
Of course, we made another date,
one that would be broke.
You stood me up so many times;
the truth you never spoke.
When I got home, I was mad at myself
for playing the fool one more time,
for not wising up to your ways.
How do I leave it all behind?
I'm not going to hang around again
in places where you may be.
I've got to try a bit harder
for you not to get the better of me.
I do not wish to see you again;
as far as I'm concerned, we never met.
So if that's the way I'm feeling now,
you'll be so easy to forget.

A Lovers' Journal

01/1980

This lovers' journal
shows a love so eternal:
Two lovers took a vow
to love each other then and now;
to hold and keep forever;
to always be together;
to make their two worlds into one;
to kiss again when day is done;
to love and cherish till death do part;
to love each other from the depths of their hearts.
Those vows, they kept their whole life long;
to each other they did belong.
In heaven, they will meet again,
because a promise is a promise
till the very end.

One Way Streets

01/1980

Wild, crazy, but sure
that I am safe and pure.
Fancy, fun, but lazy talk;
that's the street that I walk.
I only go one way

Up, up—I'll get to the top;
don't get in my way.
I don't have time to stop.
One-way streets were always alluring;
so many things we cannot do,
but many things can be done,
like when I'm alone with you.

Wicked, quiet, but very sure
if you break my heart, I have a cure.
High flying like a hawk,
that's the street that I walk.
I only go one way,
but soon I'll be there.
Don't get in my way now;
I don't have time to spare.

If I Were a Castle

01/1980

If I fly away, would you like to come along?
If I join a rock band, would you listen to my song?
If I crossed the ocean, would you take my hand?
If I said I loved you, would you understand?
If I wore tight dresses, would you look at me the same?
If I went out tonight, would you think I joined your game?
If I climbed a mountain, would you want to follow?
If I spent the night, will you love me still tomorrow?
If I were a flower, would you bring me home?
If I were a lady, would you call me your own?
If I were a radio, would you turn the volume down?
If I were a castle, would you still want me around?
If I were a wish, would you want me to come true?
And if I were in love, would you want it to be with you?

Someone Like You

02/1980

The snow was falling all around me;
the clouds were changing view.
The hope was building up inside;
I was dreaming of someone like you.
The snowy streets were lined with ice;
the sky was dark and gray,
yet that didn't matter at all to me,
because I thought you were on your way.
The temperature was dropping,
but I was filled with such desire.
As long as my heart keeps pounding,
someone like you, I so much admire.
The room is getting warmer now
since I closed the door,
but if you don't get here soon,
how will you know you're the one I adore?
The snow was piling up outside;
my tears had no place to fall.
The room is getting colder now
that I know you're not going to call.
The snow was falling all around me;
the clouds were changing view.
Once again, I sit and wonder
how I fell for someone like you.

The Forgotten Love
01/1982

It's too late; you've been gone so long,
I hardly remember your face.
I've forgotten your touch, your tender kiss,
and the feel of your warm embrace.
I have forgotten the look in your eyes
of love that is true and rare,
and I've forgotten all my dreams
that I wanted only you to share.
It's too late; you've been gone so long,
I barely remember your name.
I've forgotten the nights you held me close…
You have probably done the same.
I've forgotten the way you would hold my hand
and caress me for a while.
I forgot how much I cared;
I cannot remember your beautiful smile.
But it is too late now; you have been gone too long,
and I just cannot remember the way it was.
I have forgotten of all the good times;
I have forgotten of our love.

Remember the Love

01/1982

We've both changed in so many ways to ever go back to the way it was;
our life together is over. Please, though, do not forget the love.
Remember the nights we spent alone,
you'd take me for your very own;
you'd press your lips down on mine,
kiss me with a smile,
hold my hand, and touch my skin,
and love with me for a while.
Ever since we have been apart, we both keep changing fast;
we are strangers to each other now, so you will be my first and last.
I'll remember when we'd lay and talk, and every time, you'd hold my hand.
I'll remember the way you'd look at me and all the good things that I can.
I'll remember your face, your smile, your name;
I will not forget them never.
I'll live within the memories because now,
you're gone forever.

Fade Away
07/2019

I do not stand by your grave and weep;
I know you're not there;
I know you don't sleep.
I'm standing by your headstone,
pulling weeds up from the dirt,
remembering the day you left us,
remembering the pain, the hurt.
I'm here to water the flowers
I planted back in May;
I'm trying to recapture the memories
that seem to be fading away.
So much time has passed us by
since you've gone on to a better place.
So many years have come and gone;
I barely remember your face.
I'm sure that time does not exist,
up in heaven where you are:
there are no days, no months, no years;
there is no near; there is no far.
But here on Earth, our clocks
keep ticking away the time.
Our memories turn into dust,
and bells no longer chime.
I try hard to hold on to days of you,
and all the memories I can find.
I try so hard to keep them safe
in the corners of my mind.

Work of Art

04/1981

When rubies fall into the ocean, it's like a work of art,
reflecting the love we've come to share; I know we'll never part.
When mountains reach to touch the sky, I try to capture the view,
but still, it isn't as beautiful as my relationship with you.
When wildflowers surround the desert, the shadows are there to stay,
to remind us of our special feelings that will never slip away.
I'll grab the rainbow and hold it forever, just like a work of art,
to let you know just how much I care, and I know we will never be apart.

Your Last Goodbye

01/1982

If you never would've left me, things wouldn't have gone this way;
my mind is upside down now, and my thoughts drift every which way.
I run—around in circles; I cry—from all this pain.
I hide—trying to escape this sorrow; I dream—to keep me sane.
I write—a sad love song, then sing it to everyone,
hoping that you'll hear it and be mine again when this day is done.
If you never would've left me, I wouldn't have found someone new,
but that did not work out because every time he'd kiss me,
my eyes would only see you.
So I ran—around in circles, and cried again—from the pain.
I hid—hoping to escape the sorrow; and dreamt—to keep me sane.
Then I wrote a sad poem and sent it off to you,
hoping that you would read it and be mine again before this day was through.
But it really doesn't matter just how hard I try,
this time you're gone forever; you've said your last goodbye.

Profit From Love

01/1982

Your love for me has made me richer and made my life more complete.
Now, as I go on, there is no defeat.
As I adventure towards the future, my only desire is gentle love;
pure, sensuous, and simple, one as true as yours was.
You've poured yourself on top of me, made me richer, made me smile,
and I'll always cherish the memories of loving with you awhile.

For Rick
01/1982

Love with you, I think of gently
as I lay down to sleep.
Times of you fill my mind,
memories that I must keep.

Even the Clouds Are Crying

10/1983

Did you never like a rainy day with a gentle breeze in the air?
And can you see the leaves as they change their color and all the flowers everywhere?
Do you like the peace that surrounds you in the empty hours of the day?
And do you ever get cold and lonely and hate the cruel world that wouldn't let you stay?
I miss you now more than ever; I can't escape from all this pain.
Even the clouds are crying now, and did you never like the rain?

Memories

12/2001

So many memories: some good, some bad;
sometimes laughing, sometimes sad.
On sleepless nights, I can recall
my beginning of it all.
You were my silent hero, one to admire,
always traveling off far; you were adventure on fire.
So many memories of days gone by,
mostly we'd smile; sometimes, we'd cry.
I cherish the dreams that keep you alive through the night;
there, my hidden treasure until the daylight.
You were always nature's friend; I'd say the very best.
Now that is where you are, for your final rest.

Happy Birthday to You

03/1984

Another sunrise to greet the dawn, another day to begin,
just like the one before it, why did morning let me in?
I spent another sleepless night trying to capture memories of you,
mostly the good times we had, but there were sad times, too.
I face the world with a smile; it's only there to hide the pain.
Surely my tears will fall when I reach your new domain.
Did you know that I'd be here before this day was through?
Well, I only came to say, "Happy birthday," to you.

Love So Insane
08/1983

I've been so in love with you yet have always been alone;
where are you now while I'm lost in this world on my own?
I wait patiently as each day passes, yet I don't know what for.
I'm too scared to face the unknown future, so I hide behind my own front door.
No one ever knocked, no one ever dared;
no one came to visit, no one ever cared.
I wonder, will it always be this way, and do you still feel the pain?
And did you ever wonder why love is so insane?

Times of You
08/1983

I heard the music from the radio, I thought they were playing our song;
it brought back times of you, the only place I could ever belong.
I found an old book up in the attic, took it to bed to read;
again, it brought back times of you and a hunger that I must feed.
I've got to have you close again; I don't know which way to run.
Tears are blocking my way; I cannot feel the sun.
I'm paralyzed with the thought of not being able to touch your hands, your face;
I've forgotten how it was to be lost in your embrace.
I close my eyes to sleep, but I don't know what for.
I only dream of you and the way it was before.
Over another cup of coffee with dawn beginning to creep in,
I wonder how I lost you, when I was so sure that I could win.

Just to Say Goodbye

10/1984

If I run and call out your name, just as loud as can be;
even if it echoes in the gorge, no one will answer me.
If I plant a seed, day after day, spring will watch them grow;
there will be flowers everywhere, but you will ever know.
If I cry all day and all night in the sun and in the rain,
it's because the memories just aren't enough to let me escape the pain.
If I talk, you won't hear me, even if you really try,
but we didn't get the chance before, and I only want to say goodbye.

Simple Things
11/1983

It's the simple things I cannot find, like walking hand in hand,
or maybe seeing a rainbow, or even someone who understands.
It's the simple things I envy, like relaxing for a while,
finding time to breathe, finding time to smile.
It's the simple things I want the most, like wildflowers everywhere,
or maybe sunshine every day, or even a love you can never compare.
It's the simple things I'll never have because they are so hard to find;
it's the simple things in life that are always on my mind.

Death
11/1983

I go through the motions every day, always feeling numb inside.
Constant pain lingers there, like a part of me has died.
I see other people laughing, yet my face knows no smile,
and when they laugh too loud, I cry, but only for a while.
Every day, it's the same routine: I usually get an early start.
Sleep is hard to come by, with an empty coldness piercing my heart.
I see other people happy, but it is hard to feel that way,
because I hate this cruel world that wouldn't let you stay.

Death 2

11/1983

I search, but you're no longer there;
I hope, through all the tears,
that maybe you'll come back
and wash away my tears.
I dream you're trying to find your way;
I awake, and you're still gone.
Then I cry again;
I cry until the dawn.
I pray, over and over again;
I wonder if somehow you know.
I just don't understand,
why did you have to go?

Biding the Time

01/1984

I'm just biding my time now and going nowhere fast.
I'm too frightened to face the unknown future,
and it still hurts remembering the past.
I'm dwelling here in a place called today,
where there are certain rules as to how long one can stay.
I will not leave until I find my paradise.
Dreams just aren't enough,
for dreams cannot pave the way when the going gets too rough.
I'm just biding my time now, looking for an open door,
just trying to imagine what the future has in store.

And a Day

03/1984

You came unannounced like an April snowstorm;
you came just in time to keep me warm.
You brought the sunshine back when I thought it was gone for good,
and loving you was easy, so I loved you all I could.
You left unannounced... Why didn't you say goodbye?
You left, leaving me hanging on a thread from the sky.
You took the sunshine with you; my life turned dark and gray,
and now, you'll find me crying forever and a day.

World Beyond Compare

08/2013

Standing here at the edge of time, I can see a world beyond compare;
I'm just waiting on an angel to safely take me there.
I know that this is where I'll find, though I never had a clue,
but this is how I know that immortality is you.
You're the willow that just won't weep; you're the castle I finally found.
You're the softest breeze I feel, though you never make a sound.
Standing here at the edge of time, I can see a world we don't yet share.
I'm just waiting on an angel to safely guide me there.

I'm Not the Only One

01/1983

I thought I was the only one who could describe apathy and pain
then measure the depths of sorrow and live life in the pouring rain.
I didn't know there was anyone else who lost a love so sensuous, so true;
it never dawned on me that other eyes could cry, too.
I never really believed that someone else could hurt like me,
to grow raw and rugged like the shore before drowning out at sea.
I never imagined in my wildest dreams that good love could hurt so bad;
despair was my best friend, so cold, so cruel, so sad.
I thought I was the only one who ever felt just plain blue,
always numb and empty inside, until the day that I met you.
You were like I was looking at my shadow, just waiting to be set free;
reflections in your eyes showed that you were just like me.
Running through time, trying to escape from scars that just won't heal,
forgotten how to love again; forgotten how to feel.
Now, a photograph is all that is left of times we tried to share.
Old sorrow got in our way though and told us not to care.
I thought I was the only one who lost a love thought so true,
I didn't know anyone else had eyes that could cry, too.

Gates of Hell
01/1985

The gates of hell have opened wide and set me free once more
out into a place called love, but I've been here before.

Always hits me like a bullet, hard, and also very fast;
now, scars are all that's left. Love never seems to last.

It rips me into pieces and leaves me crying for a while;
tears are all that is left from a face that knows no smile.

Each time, it leaves me colder, more bitter words to tell;
love always leads me back to the rusted gates of hell.

Time Away

01/1985

Here I am, just time away, not knowing where to start.
I want to say I'm sorry, and I hate each moment we are apart.
I'd like to feel your breath warm my skin, get lost in love for a while;
I want to be near you again, to drown myself within your smile.
I want to hold you closer now than I ever have before;
I want to be with you again. I want to be with love once more.
Still, I'm here just time away, missing you so much.
I want to have you close again; I want to feel your touch.

Ruins

01/1985

I'm running through fields of half-forgotten dreams,
the ones I know will never come true.
They're torn and shattered, just like me,
and they're gone forever, just like you.
I thought we'd always be together;
I thought you really cared.
It was in the way you'd touch me;
it was in the love we shared.
I'm tripping through the ruins of dreams
that I know are gone for good.
You left me stranded on the edge of love;
you left me, right after you promised you never would.

Heaven
01/1985

I want to hold you till the ocean runs dry,
until the mountains crumble and are gone,
until all time just fades away,
until it's night and never dawn.
I want to kiss you till we just can't breathe,
until the sparks all catch fire,
until we both just melt away,
until we reach a place called desire.
I want to love you now and forever,
until the stars fall from the sky,
until wild flowers surround the dessert,
until we're in heaven, just you and I.

Upon a Star
12/2011

The desires we share will take us everyplace we wish to go.
Our paradise is near; let's hop upon a star
and travel far away from here.
The passion that I hold for you is far beyond compare.
You're drowning in my powers; touch me if you dare.
I cannot find escape from the hold you have on me;
you're everything I've dreamed—don't ever set me free.
Run faster; now, I'm waiting. There is a star falling our way.
Jump on with me if you dare and on to a better day.

Day by Day
01/1984

I'm the unicorn that stands on the hill; no one knows I'm real.
No one lives nearby; alone is how it makes me feel.
I search, as far as I can see, for someone who will care.
Yet I have never seen, anyone ever, anywhere.
Lost in this world by myself with no one to betray,
I'm the unicorn on the hill, living my life day by day.

Starry Nights

01/1984

I dedicate to you a starry night and the wonder of it all,
the perfect image of heaven, the beauty I still recall.
Hold it; don't ever let it go because it will never come again;
it's a once in a lifetime dream, and dreams like this one end.
But I dedicate to you this starry night, a world beyond eternity,
a place to let your fears escape yet keep in touch with reality.

To Say Goodbye

02/1984

Winter kept me far from here, but it won't keep me away no more;
now, it's time to stay forever by the lakeshore.
This place is possessing me, telling me never to let go,
or vanish back into this cruel world that I have come to know.
The tide tries to reach out to grab me, so it can pull me far away from here,
maybe as far as serenity, where all apathy would disappear.
The depth of the sand slows me down till I can no longer run and cry,
but I never got the chance before, and I only want to say goodbye.

Memorial Day This Year

05/1984

On this early morning in May, my tears are blinding me.
Your name is not in lights, but it is all that I can see.
I'm here to say a prayer for you, to remember how good it's been;
now, it's so sad to even think how we lost one so genuine.
Today is for the memories that have forbidden us to sleep.
It's to unfair to even understand why we stand by your grave and weep.
On this early morning in May, I try hard not to cry,
but the tears are blinding me, now that I've come to say goodbye.

An August Morning

08/1984

A year ago, this August morning, God took you away,
leaving only memories; grief is the debt we now pay.
We are trying hard to remember just how good it's been,
but it's just too sad to even think how we lost one so genuine.
We cherish the dreams that keep you alive through the night,
they're our hidden treasure until the daylight.
On this early August morning, we say another prayer for you,
and when we've said goodbye, we'll ask for God to see us through.

On Christmas Day This Year

12/1984

December nights are long and cold; winter is just a breath away.
It's the saddest of times, I know; it's almost Christmas Day.
Memories of you come alive as this season makes me blue,
and it's still so hard to even understand how we lost one so true.
I see other people laughing, though I've forgotten how.
Everyone is as joyful as the season, but that is hard to do right now.
Instead, I say another prayer that I hope somehow you'll hear,
so you'll know you're in our hearts on Christmas Day this year.

Never

04/1985

Never sad, never happy, never any fun;
that's the way life goes, much easier said than done.
Never laugh, never smile, just forgotten how.
Too long to remember, hurting is all I know right now.
Never warm, never cold; just plain numb inside.
Life goes on and on, though I feel I've already died.
Never content; never bitter; there is nothing I can feel,
only emptiness forever in a heart that just won't heal.

Shades of Death

08/1985

Two years ago on this day, God took you very far away;
He led you to a place called home, up in heaven, where angels roam.
No more life; no more love; all is gone, what you were dreaming of.
Was it hard letting go to where endless time is all you know?
Is it warm, or is it cold? Maybe lonesome with no one to hold?
What is it like where you are? Do you feel close to home, yet so far?
Can you still feel? What can you do? Can you see me? I wish I knew.
What happened to the life you had all planned?
Why is death so hard to understand?

Death 3

01/1986

Death is the enemy that lurks in the shadows, following us
where ever we go. Always there, waiting to reach out and grab us;
to pull us down with it.
Death is the stranger that patiently waits, eager to catch us by
surprise. Always there, watching with eyes that want to make us friends forever.
Death is the law that forbids us to live on, insisting we all abide.
Always there, waiting with handcuffs, ready to lock us up forever.

The Graveyard by the Gorge

05/1988

I pull the weeds from your grave and put flowers in their place;
soon, they, too, will be dead—gone without a trace.
Is there really a heaven? Did you find your paradise?
Can you see? Can you feel? And is it very nice?
Or is it cold? Is it dark? Is there never any sound?
Are you bitter? Are you numb? Is it hell to be buried in the ground?
I pulled the weeds from your grave and put flowers there for you;
the brightest colors of spring, I hope that you can see them, too.

When I Call Out Your Name

09/1990

Every time I see a pick-up truck or someone six feet tall,
every time I hear the radio playing "Meatloaf" or "The Wall,"
each time I see old photographs, I'm reminded of before,
only now, there is no answer when I knock upon your door.
Every time I see a folk guitar or hear Randy's "Old 8x10,"
each time I see a carrot cake, your memory floods my mind again.
The days pass, and life goes on, but it can never be the same
because now you just don't answer when I call out your name.

November Nights, Version 2

11/1993

For John

November nights are long and cold; winter is just a breath away.
Memories of you fill our hearts on this very special day.
Every time I see a pick-up truck or someone six-foot tall,
every time I hear the radio playing Travis or "The Wall,"
each time we look at photos or see one of your friends,
each time we cook a turkey, we think of you once again.
And tonight, when we say our prayers, we hope, somehow, you'll hear,
so you'll know you're in our hearts on your birthday this year.

Heaven's Door, Version 2

06/1991

For John

One full year has passed us by since God took you away,
leaving only memories that we treasure every day.
Is there really a heaven? Did you find your paradise?
Are there flowers, maybe music? And is it very nice?
What is it like where you are? Do you feel close to home, yet so far?
Can you still feel? What can you do? Can you see me? I wish I knew.
If I knocked on heaven's door, could you hear or would you try?
Because we never got the chance before, and I only wish to say goodbye.

For Marge
02/1984

One full year has passed us by, and now we have no more tears to cry,
so memories of you, we will gather up, and we'll keep them like a treasure.
We all miss you so much; depths an angel could not measure.
You'll be in our hearts forever; every day, and nighttime, too.
And on this winter's evening, we say another prayer for you.

Seldom

01/1986

Seldom, he sees me where I am seated at the edge of his sight, refusing to look further my way. Seldom, he hears me as I scream softly throughout the day—a little louder during the night.

He doesn't understand me; patience is totally unknown. He's as cold as the winter months, even together we are alone.

Seldom, he feels me as I struggle to hold him near. Scorched with desire, and he still won't touch. Seldom, he needs me as I need him, and yet I love him very much.

Black

04/1986

Spring time is simple and nice; it brings all beauty back to life.
We look easy; it's breath taking. We soak it in, plant it in our soul,
engrave it in our mind, and we think it'll stay with us forever.
But then, one day, suddenly, death strikes and pulls us down,
and straps us there, not even giving us one last breath, and all the beauty
of life we were so sure we'd never forget is gone—never to be seen again.
Everything now is silent and black.

Some Days
04/1984

You don't ask how I've been, or what I have been doing
since the day you walked out that door.
You don't know where I'm going or what I've been feeling
since you don't love me anymore.
You don't care if I'm hurting or if I've been crying
because the pain is just too much to bare
You don't know if I'm living, though my heart is slowly dying
since you left me with only despair.
Some days are lonely now; some days are really long.
Some days just leave me chilled right to the bone.
Some days are hard now; some days I am just numb
since you left me here so all alone.

Traveling Man
06/1989

I met him in the winter time, almost a year ago,
passing through this snowy town, traveling rather slow.
He stopped into the local diner to order coffee, the take-out kind,
then he'd be on the road again, leaving this place far behind.
I knew I could not let that happen—I had to learn his name.
Somehow, I knew as I approached him, my life would never be the same.
He joined me in a corner booth; we talked the afternoon away.
Then I asked him softly, if maybe he would stay.
"For just a little while," he said, "a week or maybe more."
After the time we spent together, I knew I'd never be as I was before.
He stayed to keep me warm, many cold and sleepless nights.
We loved the hours away; I held on so very tight.
The winter months passed us by; scents of spring were in the air.
I didn't think he'd ever leave behind a love so precious, so rare.
But he's on the road again; he's a traveling man—you see,
even though the roads belong to him, his heart belongs to me.

Ashland City, Tennessee
07/1989

Driving down this country road, it's in my blood, I've got to see
the legend I've been dreaming of, here in Ashland City, Tennessee.
I know you from the radio, pouring your heart out in your songs,
sharing your deepest, darkest feelings, being so gentle, yet so strong.
From the first time I heard your voice, I've wanted to touch your face, kiss your smile,
feel your warmth upon my skin, and love with you for a little while.
I've traveled many lonely miles, just to make my dream come true.
I'm not sure yet just what I'll say when finally I meet you;
I don't even know what I might do when you open up your door.
Could you like me as I like you? Is there a chance for something more?
I cannot predict the future or what fate has in mind for me.
The only thing that I am sure of, is that my heart lives here, in Ashland City, Tennessee

Color Me Gone

04/1991

It was more than love, my feelings for you,
and I honestly thought you felt it, too.
I was lost in your love; safe in your arms,
so deep in your heart, I was shielded from harm.
I gave it my all, my last breath, my last sigh—
I gave you my soul; you bled it dry.
Now, my body is numb, my heartbeat, so still;
and the sound of my pain rings through the hills.
The hurt lives on; I'm darker than dawn,
so alone and so empty. Please, just color me gone.

If Dreams Came True

01/1984

I remember the good; sometimes the bad,
and I'll always remember all the love we had.
I remember talking, yet nothing was said.
We showed our feelings through touching instead.
I remember laughing every now and then,
and all the bittersweet things when I can.
I remember you leaving, although you never said goodbye
And I remember running home to cry.
I remember now: Dreams don't always come true,
because if they did, then surely, I'd still be with you.

Softer Than the Moonlight
11/1981

All the rainbows are falling from heaven and landing by my feet,
surrounding me with beauty, and filling up the empty streets.
Waves are rolling into shore to try to catch a different view;
they drift among the silky sands, then I drift home to you.
I run into your outstretched arms and hide within your smile,
bury myself upon your very touch, and love with you for a little while.
Roses of red, yellow, and white are blooming now, one by one,
to scent the air along the way as they try to reach the sun.
I listen to the radio that plays some tunes that I once knew;
I drown within the music, but once I escape, I'm back with you.
I'm back in your arms that bring me warmth; I'm still hiding within your smile.
Your touch is softer than the moonlight when I love with you for a little while

He Killed Me

11/1981

His kisses were always tender; I'd melt upon his touch.
I'd lay within his warmth until he killed me, yet he loved me very much.
I'd try to keep him smiling, caress him with my gentle touch;
I ached for his skin upon mine until he killed me, yet I love him very much.

A Little Longer

11/1980

He was here, but there he goes—they're always gone before you know.
My love was strong, and growing stronger,
if he would just come back and stay a little bit longer.
He was alone, but then I came; I made him happy; I was the same.
I was laughing; he liked my smile, if he'd just come back and stay a little while.
He was singing a song to me, and I listened patiently. It was a love song I heard before;
now, if he'd just come back and sing it just once more.
He was here, but now he's gone. They always leave before the dawn.
My love was strong and getting stronger; now,
if he'd just come back and stay a little bit longer.

Portrait of You

01/1981

Painting pictures in my dreams of a man who used to love me,
a portrait of you with a beautiful face and a wonderful warm embrace,
with big, bright eyes that only show just how much you love me so.
But then my paintings blew away, but I don't really care.
Because they were so beautiful, the memory will always be there.
And that is not really so bad because my whole life through
will be made of memories, and the best will be of you.

The Rubber Flowers Are Missing

01/1980

I used to have some pretty flowers that stuck to the bottom of my tub,
so I would never slip and fall.
Then one day, I came home from working late
and couldn't find those flowers anywhere at all.
Then I asked my sister to come and help me look around,
but the flowers from the tub were nowhere to be found.
We asked our friends and neighbors, but they didn't really care;
some of them even said that, "Them flowers were never really there."
But we know they were because the glue left on the bottom of the tub was still
kinda sticky; they just told us to get some more and not to be so picky.
Where did the flowers out of my bathtub go?
It's been six long years, and still I'd like to know.

Young and Beautiful

01/1980

She was young and pretty and maybe a little naïve;
she had promised her lover that she would never leave.
He was tall and handsome; he took everything in stride.
He never thought his lover would ever leave his side.
They ate then danced by candlelight, made their two worlds into one;
so many times, they'd sit and talk, long after day was done.
He knew that he was looking good, and the girls all looked his way,
and the flattery took over; no hesitation or delay.
He said that he was working late, which his lover could not believe.
Why did she promise him that she would never leave?
She put all her faith in him after the vows they silently spoke,
but he took her trust away. Would her heart be permanently broke?
They both went their separate ways; their worlds are now so far apart.
She couldn't forgive her lover for breaking up her heart.
She was young and pretty; she had so much to give.
And when the scars finally heal, she can begin to again live.

Blooms

06/2015

I pull the weeds from your grave and put flowers in their place;
all the colors of summer: red, purple, orange, and maize.
I lay in the grass beside your headstone and gaze up at the sky,
watching the clouds take on different form as they lazily drift on by.
I'm here to spend the day with you and to tell you just how I feel.
It's been 25 long years now, and I know my broken heart will never heal.
I think of times so long ago, the winters and the summers we had,
the picnics, the parks, swings and sleds, back when we didn't know the meaning of sad.
Did you know that I'd be here before this day was through?
Because I only wanted to say just how much I'm missing you.

Heaven
06/2015

If I could go back in time and change just one thing,
it would be that summer night in June because of all the pain that it would bring.
I would take the bad guys out of the picture and place you on the beach alone,
enjoying a peaceful summer's evening with a drink and an ice cream cone.
Days to follow would be filled with joy, picnics, parks, family, and friends,
but God had another plan He did not share. We didn't know how it all would end.
He sent down some angels to guide you to a new place you now call home,
so far away from the ones who love you; you're up in heaven where the angels roam.
So, if I could change just one thing, it would be the day you died.
It would be the never-ending pain, and all the tear my eyes have cried.

Paper Dress
02/1980

No one listens, no one hears, all my dreams, all my fears;
No one talks, no one laughs, at the future or the past;
No one smiles, no one cries, except for me—you've said goodbye.
I walk along in paper dress, words are sloppy, hair's a mess.
No one sees, no one cares, no one will stop and stare;
No one wants, no one needs, when I sell my flower seeds;
No one has come, no one has gone—I'm here alone again at dawn.
No one hurts or feels any pain except for me when you are vain.
I walk along this silent street, wearing nothing on my feet.
I talk out loud, but no one hears. I must have cried a million tears
I walk alone, dragging my chair; I get to you, but you don't care
No one sees, yet they're not blind. They only wonder why you left me behind.

I'm a Writer

11/1980

The sky was falling down around me, I've lost all piece of mind;
I've cried enough to make an ocean, because you, my love, I'm leaving behind.
The world is closing in on me; flowers are dying one by one,
and still, I'll have nothing to show when morning comes and brings the sun.
This city is the same, day after day; I'm the only one who is changing fast,
and now I've got a dream to catch—not my first and not my last.
I'm a writer, and one day soon, everyone will know.
I'm a writer, and through my words, rainbows will grow.
The clouds are falling down around me; traffic lights are red, then green.
People get up; they go to work; every day is the same routine.
The music is playing all around me; I walk the streets, mile after mile.
I'm only going to catch a dream; I'll be back, my love, in just a while.
I'm a writer, and one day soon, everyone will see
that jets and tinsel clothes are just another side of me.

Don't You Remember?

11/1980

My phone isn't ringing off the wall; there is no one knocking at my door.
Your smile is just a memory of how I lived before.
Your face is just a dark gray cloud that brings on the rain,
and the puddles that I'm stepping in once washed away the pain.
Don't you remember you said you loved me?
Don't you remember you said you cared?
And on those long, cold, lonely nights,
don't you remember the love we shared?
Your name is just another name, maybe I have heard before;
our song is just another song I don't wish to hear no more.
Your touch is now as cold as ice, though once it warmed my heart, my mind;
your kisses were a winter's fire, now they're so hard to find.
Don't you remember you said you loved me?
Don't you remember you said you care?
And on those long, cold, lonely nights,
don't you remember I'm no longer there?

Love Song
01/1981

I wrote a sad song when I was feeling down,
hoping that you'd hear it, and you would come around.
But it didn't matter to you that the whole nation cried;
you sat by yourself and took it all in stride.
I wrote a love song, just hoping to see
if you heard it enough that you'd follow me.
But it didn't matter at all that the whole nation heard,
you sat there all alone; never mumbled a word.
I wrote a joyful song, especially for you,
hoping that you'd hear it before the day was through.
But it didn't really matter that the whole nation sang it, too, still,
you sat there alone drinking up your brew.
So then I wrote one more song that filled the nation with laughter,
wishing that you'd hear it and be mine ever after.
But it didn't matter to you just how hard I tried;
you still sat there by yourself and took it all in stride.

Military Man
07/1981

In my dream, Ron was waving goodbye;
alone I stood very still and cried.
In my dream, Ron was leaving;
he was flying over the sea.
He left behind most of his belongings;
he also left behind me.
In my dream, Ron was running;
he had to catch a plane.
In my dream, he was running fast,
trying to beat the rain.
In my dream, Ron was waving goodbye,
then he was on his way.
Ron, didn't you just get home?
Wasn't that just yesterday?

Forever?

09/1981

The way you hug and kiss me, I know we'll always be together;
and the way you love me tenderly is like saying that we are forever.
You're all I'll ever want; you're the only one who can love me this way;
you're all I'll ever need in all my tomorrows and today.
You are my inspiration and a dream come true;
there is no one else I could ever love the way that I love you.
It's in the way you touch me, the feeling is oh so rare,
and I know that I will never drift beyond your love and care.

The Lily Pond

07/1981

I'm another lily in this pond; to you, I am unknown.
I lie in this water, just looking nice; all day, I'm all alone.
There is a weeping willow bending over me,
the sky is a paler shade of blue;
after dark, all that is left behind
is a wet covering of dew.
Then I wake up, and the dream is gone.
I'm still sitting here all alone,
looking out over the lily pond,
my secret place of my very own.

If

10/1981

If there were a million rainbows in the sky
and a thousand sailboats out at sea,
if the clouds were outlined with diamonds
would you still think of me?
If there were rubies in the desert
and the scent of roses filled the air,
if there were a place called paradise,
would you take me there?
If there were wild flowers on the moon
and seahorses on the shore,
if all the stars fell from the sky,
would you bring me more?
If the Milky Way was a place we could visit
and Disneyland was something new,
if serenity was around the corner,
I'd only want to go there with you.

There You Go

02/1980

There you go, here am I, looks as though you're waving goodbye.
There you are, just going home, here am I, on my own.
There you are, driving into the night, I can see the red tail lights.
There you are, without a care; here am I, with dreams to share.
There you go, you're on your way; here I stand, here I stay.
There you go, on a cloud; here I mix with the crowd.
There you go, with your smile; did you know I like your style?
There you go, headed for home; here am I, lost and alone.
There you go, but here am I, looks like you are waving goodbye.

Look Out
02/1980

I was daydreaming, burning like a flame,
running hot and wild, then you came.
I was falling, down a steep, rocky hill;
when I hit the bottom, there you were, silent and still.
I was losing something I had won;
when I made a move, I turned, and you were gone.
I was walking down a dead-end street.
When I got to you, you stepped on my feet.
I was crying; the tears flowed down my face.
When they finally stopped, you were gone without a trace.
I was dizzy, so sick of feeling blue;
every time I stopped turning, I had to laugh at you.
I was singing, a song that has no end.
When you heard the melody, you stepped on my feet again.
I was daydreaming, burning like the sun;
you hurt me once too often. Look out now, here I come.

Words
02/1980

This paper was empty until I picked up a pen,
and the words I am writing cannot be written again.
The mountains are rugged yet can't be defined,
like under water caves and days far behind.
Love is like a jewel you can never describe,
like the ocean at night, or an old Indian tribe.
Stars are like treasures that sparkle in the sky;
words are for writing; words never die.
People are faces that get lost in a crowd;
they all blend together like thousands of clouds.
Men are for loving; that's the way it should be,
and if it only happens once, that is enough for me.

Pretend

02/1980

I don't dream anymore; I've forgotten how to sleep.
I don't swim anymore; the waters got too deep.
I don't write anymore; the words come out the same.
I don't build fires anymore; the wind blows out the flame.
Sometimes, I pretend I am a bluebird, trapped up in the sky;
no one can take my wings away—over the oceans, I fly.

Sometimes, I want to hate you and drown you out at sea.
Sometimes, I want to love you and hold you tenderly.
Sometimes, I pretend I am an angel, trapped within the sky.
No one can take my halo away—through the heavens I fly.

I don't pretend anymore; I think I've forgotten how.
I'll never again be a butterfly, but that's all right for now.

I Write This Poem for You

04/1980

I wrote a poem last summer; someone else wrote one, too,
but mine was filled with sorrow. You see, it was for you.
I've written poems of joy and flowers hard to find;
I've also wrote some sad things when you were on my mind.
I've written poems of waters that run wild, very deep;
I've written poems of mountains I could not climb—they were too steep.
I wrote a poem last fall; it was very hard to do.
My poem was filled with sadness; you see, it was for you.
I've written poems of ships and rainbows after a storm,
and I wrote a poem of happiness after a night you kept me warm.
I wrote a poem last winter about someone I once knew,
but that poem was filled with tears; you see, it was for you.
I've written poems of wonder, hope and fame, ice and snow;
I've written poems of dreams I've had; some I kept, but others, I let go.
I wrote a poem to begin the spring, the world looked brand-new,
but my poem was filled with anguish. Again, it was for you.
I've written poems of rivers and mountains, trying to touch the sky above;
I've written poems for friends of mine, and I've written poems of love.
I wrote a poem to begin my day; someone else wrote one, too,
but mine was filled with gloom. You see, it was for you.

A Million Years

05/1980

You came while I was crying, made a smile drown the tears;
I really thought my smile would last for at least a million years.
You left while I was laughing; my joy turned into sorrow.
I thought the pain would never end; how could I face tomorrow?
You came while the sun was shining, took it with you when you went away…
Dark clouds are hanging over me now, as I slip back to yesterday.
There, I capture the memories, and the beauty that we shared,
and all the times that I told you just how much I really cared.
I relive the times we spent together; the kisses that turned to fire;
late night walks along the beach, all the things I so desire.
You came while I was sad; let a smile replace my frown.
I thought it was forever—I never thought you'd let me down.
You left while I was happy, made my smile turn to tears;
and now, you'll find me crying for a least a million years.

Red Rose

A red rose in a crystal vase
lives in a world with no one to face.
But me, I face strangers every day;
I face strangers in every way.
It scares me to know you're not around;
it scares me to know you can't be found.
A rose needs water to stay alive;
I need you to survive.
It's tough, facing people in a society
where you do not belong;
it's rough when you know
you're not that strong.
But I could be if I had you
to see me through in everything I do.

Portrait

Painting pictures in my dreams of a man whom used to love me,
a portrait of you with a beautiful face and a wonderful, warm embrace,
you have that smile I used to know. I still wonder, why did you go?

You, Once Again

Every time I start to cry, it's you who makes me smile;
every time I get ready to go, it's you who makes me stay a while.
For every day of pain, I have two days of sun;
every time I kiss you, I feel my life has just begun.
Each time I fall off to sleep, I dream you're next to me,
And each time that I awake, it's you, once again.

I Saw Him Through the Mist

I watched the waves come up along the shore, and he was at my side;
I watched the smile upon his face when he came in, it was hard to hide.
I wait for him in my dreams each night soon after I fall to sleep.
I wait for him at my front door, knowing his love is mine to keep.
We love to laugh and sing; we do everything together.
I will be his girl forever; he will be my man. I will leave him never.
I look into the mist, knowing he'll be there.
I look into the clear blue sky, knowing this love, we will always share.

Reflections on the Wonders of This World

Wonder is an aura of beauty that appears overhead and then suddenly dissolves into space.
Wonder is the feeling you get when looking deeply into one's own beautiful face.
Wonder is the reflection of a fire that has an everlasting blaze.
Wonder is God, who always works in mysterious ways.
Wonder is a tornado that, at any minute, can come twirling around a bend.
Wonder is how this amazing world doesn't have any end.
Wonder is the fulfillment and knowledge you give to yourself
and everyone who passes you by.
Wonder is not always knowing the answer to the question, "Why?"

Treasured Times

04/1987

The years were slowly slipping by; love would come, love would go;
never lasting long at all, love would die instead of grow.
The months were passing, one by one; winter was knocking at my door,
bringing yet another chance at love, maybe different than the ones before.
Trees were budding, flowers blooming; a scent of spring was in the air.
Watching nature bring back life was just the beginning of what we'd share.
All the months that passed me by, the endless days I felt so blue.
The long, cold nights, I spent alone were all worth the wait for you.
Your love is all I hoped for, bigger than any mountain one could climb,
and every moment we've spent together is a precious, treasured time.

Way Back When
10/1991

I had forgotten your hands, your face; your name had slipped my mind.
I no longer knew your gentle touch; those days I had left behind.
The years passed by; time went on. I was living a whole new life.
I had a job; I had a baby. I was living a whole new life.
Days of you were long since gone; I couldn't remember the love we shared.
Times of you were put to rest, until I turned around and saw you there.
Suddenly, thoughts of you flooded my mind; old feelings rushed in so strong.
I couldn't stop the past from coming back, even though it was wrong.
It was like I was 16 all over again, lost in the love we once knew,
and when I looked into your eyes, I could tell you felt the same way, too.
We talked and laughed for a while; we kept the conversation light,
though all I really wanted was for you to hold me tight.
I came home alone that evening though I was missing you so much,
hurting inside all over again; I was longing for your touch.
But you're not a part of my life now, and never will be again;
so all I have left of you are my memories from way back when.

Feel For You

11/1994

If you were a million miles away, I'd probably still feel the same,
because my heart skips a beat whenever I hear your name.
My hands begin to shake; my knees get very weak;
my brain just freezes up, so I can barely speak.
I want to reach out and touch you every time that you walk by,
and if I ever kissed you, I just know that I would die.
But this is just a dream I have, a wish that won't come true,
because you don't feel for me the way that I feel for you.

11/1994

If I could have just one of all my dreams come true,
I'd hop upon the softest cloud and float away with you.
I'd take you to the moon and back; I'd take you out to sea.
I'd take you to a place called heaven; I'd take you there with me.
We can find our paradise—the stars will guide us there,
where the sky is always blue, and roses scent the air.
If I had just one dream that really could come true,
I'd want to be with love again; I'd want to be with you.

Gates of Hell, Part II

03/1995

The gates of hell have opened up to let me out once more,
so far away from a place called love; well, I've been here before.
I'm back inside this dungeon, trapped within these walls of sorrow,
wounded deep from mountains of pain, looking for a better tomorrow.
The walls are crashing in on me; my only friend is now despair,
so cold, so cruel, so sad. This heartache beyond repair.
I'm not sure which way to turn; grief is my best friend.
Drowning in this dungeon of apathy, never to see the gardens again.
The gates of hell have opened up and dared me to step inside,
down into a cold, cruel place, where emptiness and heart break hide.

From Fire to Ashes

02/1995

I know your face; I know your smile.
I know your walk; I like your style.
I know your touch and your heartbeat.
I feel desire; I feel heat.
I know your eyes and how you see.
I liked the way you'd look at me.
I know your voice; I like the sound.
I'm on fire when you're around.
I know the good; I know the bad.
I know it's over, what we had.
I knew it was over when I saw your face,
and there would never be another embrace.
I knew you'd leave; I just knew you would,
and I'd forget you now if I could.
I knew it was ending when you said goodbye.
I knew it would hurt; I knew I would cry.
I knew I'd feel empty; I knew I'd be sad.
I knew that love can hurt so bad.
I knew the word "sorrow" and what it could do,
but I never dreamed it would come from you.
I thought that you loved me; I thought it was true.
But now, it is over; now, we are through.

If God Were a Woman

02/1995

Not long ago, my life was right, and love was knocking at my door.
I thought we were so perfect; I wanted nothing more.
The desire I felt deep inside, the passion I felt for you
made me think that maybe God was a woman, too.
But if God were a woman, I wouldn't hurt so bad.
Life would be happy, not so empty and sad.
If God were a woman, I'd be there, loving you;
she'd make all my wishes and dreams come true.
If God were a woman, we'd be together today;
you'd be here loving me, and forever you'd stay.

Autumn Breeze

02/1982

I'd like to hop up on a windy night and travel very far away,
lose myself in a gentle breeze, forget the heartbreak of yesterday.
I'd like to leap into a cottony cloud or fall into the rainbow's end,
maybe lose myself in a pot of gold and try to forget of you again.
I'd like to be up on a mountain top, closer to the sky and sun;
lose myself in a gentle breeze, maybe cry again when day is done.
I'd like to be by the sandy shore and maybe watch the tide come in,
throw my thoughts of you into the ocean, but where do I begin?
I'd like to sail in to a gust of night or disappear into eternity;
anything to forget you, maybe lose myself in an autumn breeze.

That Old Photograph
06/1983

I wish I could've talked to you, kissed you and held you close;
then I saw that old photograph, and I thought I was seeing a ghost.
It's been so long since I've touched you; I wish that you could be here.
Then I looked at that old photograph, and suddenly, you were very clear.
My memories were so very vivid of the love we used to share,
and I never dreamed I'd ever drift beyond your love and care.
I truly thought you felt for me in the depths of your heart;
all the passion of the world and till eternity, we'd never part.
When I stared at that old photograph, I noticed the coldness in your face;
then it didn't take too long before you were gone without a trace.
With all the hell you put me through, this love I hold for you won't die,
and in that old photograph, I can see now, you're waving goodbye.

Me Without You

02/1983

I'm sure the stars are probably easier to reach than you are;
you're like a cloud, trying to catch a runaway rainbow.
Maybe even like an autumn storm, it comes and then it goes.
Starfish are easier to find than you, and dreams aren't all the same;
they are like the birds in the sky—each one has a name.
Some dreams are easier to remember than you are;
mountains are easier to climb; the desert is hot and dry.
I think the Earth is running out of time.
I'm sure the sun is easier to touch than you are,
maybe heaven is for real, and didn't someone, somewhere say
a broken heart will never heal?

Please Don't Write a Sad Song

02/1982

If those words get tangled with music, the reality of why
they were written would vanish fast,
and then I'd be reminded time and time again of
all the heart break in my past.
Every time I'd hear that song,
I'd see your face, your smile;
I'd feel your breath upon my lips and
remember loving with you for a while.
I'd be able to hear your voice calling my name,
so real, I'd almost be able to touch you.
So, please, don't write a sad song,
because I'm already feeling blue.
Every time I heard that song,
my heart would break again.
I'd remember you said, "We'll always be together,
I'll love you, Honey, until the end."
I'd be able to feel your warmth upon my skin
so real, I'd almost want to cry,
and I'd be reminded once again
that you really did say goodbye.
I'd think of the love I held for you,
so strong, it was almost insane.
So, please, don't write a sad song,
because I couldn't bear the pain.

Alone, but With the Sounds
02/1982

I'm sitting here alone again; alone, but with the sounds
of cars and trucks and buses, music far in the background.
I want to leave this noisy room and find a quiet place
far beyond serenity, far from the human race.
I'd like to rest myself upon a cloud, feel the softness warm me through,
cradle myself within its white, and pretend that it was you.
I'd like to put myself within your reach, touch your skin, feel your face,
press my lips down on yours, and love with you in a quiet place.
But I'm sitting here alone again, with nothing but the sounds
of sirens, people and traffic, music far in the background.

Someday

02/1982

Even though I love you now, it won't always be this way;
there will come a time I will forget you—I will forget, one day.
I'll forget the time that you weren't there,
promises you made yet never kept,
the fights that would last for days on end,
the nights I cried but should've slept.
I'll forget the good times along with the bad,
like the sensation of your touch,
the way you'd hold me tenderly when I needed it so much.
I know this hurt will go away, the heartbreak over losing you,
but these feelings of love won't go away; at least not until I do.
Even though I love you now, it won't always be this way.
There is going to be a time I will forget you
when I die, someday.

Once More

03/1982

I can't remember ever feeling the way I did while we were together;
it's impossible to put in words, I had hoped it would last forever.
I ached inside when you left; I didn't believe time would heal this pain.
My love for you ran deep, so pure that it was insane.
Other men now come and go, but the feeling is never the same;
my only desire is to see your face and to remember love by name.
I often wonder if it's this way with you; do you miss me? Do you care?
Is your smile hiding the pain? Do you want me to be there?
I want to feel those feelings again, just as I did before;
I want to be with love again. I want to be with you once more.

The Waiting

04/1982

I'm still waiting for you to come back, so we can be as we were before;
I'll wait forever if I have to, just to hold you close once more.
I fell in love with you once; that feeling never went away.
I'll wait my lifetime if I have to; I'll love you forever and a day.
I'm going to make you mine again; somehow, there is a way, I'm sure.
You, Hon, are the catch, and I am the lure.
I painted love on my fingertips and poured some in the wine,
so the next time I touch you, I know that you'll be mine.
I have always loved you, and of course, I always will.
If it takes a hundred years for you to come back, you'll find me waiting still.

Cry

04/1982

I cried so hard when you said goodbye; I didn't fight the tears.
I couldn't imagine how life would be without you through the years.
I tried so hard to hang on, but you kept pushing me away;
I couldn't imagine anything worse than living off memories of yesterday.
What I wanted more than anything else was for you to come and hold me tight,
Then, with my skin soft against yours, tell me everything would be alright.
I tried real hard to keep you happy, I really tried to make you proud.
I never even imagined how it would be to cry out loud.
Well, I cried so hard when you left, I couldn't fight the tears
because I imagined how life would be without you through the years.

Remember Me

05/1982

Remember me? I showed you love and all that it meant;
I touched your face, your heart, I gave my all, myself to you.
I'm so lost while we're apart.
I miss your skin warm on mine, more than you'll ever understand;
I miss everything about you. I love you more than anybody else can.
Remember me? I gave you love and all that it meant;
desire was you and I, if we had enough to last a lifetime
then why did we say goodbye?
Remember me as the years go on, until all eternity,
until the mountains crumble and are gone, just remember me.

Without You

05/1982

So long now, without love, I just can't remember the joy, the bliss;
I've forgotten the sadness that walks with it also.
Feeling simply nothing, I'm like a rock, or a hole that knows no depth,
clouds at a standstill, a smile that knows no face.
Always the same: never sad; never happy.
Time without you has left me just plain empty.
I love you, but too late; together we love, apart, I hate.
Your touch is my tranquilizer; your absence is my destiny;
your love is my desire.

Killing Me

06/1982

There you are miles away, killing me, and the pain is just too much;
I want to have you close again; my desire is your touch.
You are forever on my mind; I always feel your presence near.
There is no doubt in my mind, one day soon, you'll be right here,
then I can reach out and hold you and love you till we break,
drown within our passion every moment that we're awake.
Why are you miles away, just killing me? The pain is never-ending.
I want to feel you close again; I can't go on pretending.
You are forever on my mind; desire is where I'm from,
and being alone without you now has left me just plain numb.

He Died Today

06/1982

He no longer has a need for me; it's obvious he doesn't care.
No matter how I feel, he will no longer be there.
In my mind, he died today; I heard it in his voice.
This isn't the way it should be, but I don't have a choice.
He's never coming back; he's tired of my face…
This love he threw away can never be replaced.
He no longer has a need for me, even though I love him more
than I did yesterday or even the day before.
My life is empty without him; I wish that he would stay,
but I must accept he is gone now. In my mind, he died today.

Years From Now

06/1982

Perhaps in years to come, after my sorrow has had time to fade away,
you and I will meet once more.
We'll talk a while, then see the changes we've been through and wonder
if we can love as we did before.
Perhaps in years from now, after my heart has completely healed, you and
I will meet once more, or
maybe I'll find someone new; maybe you will, too, then we'll know that we
just can't love like we did before.

Possessed

06/1983

I'm possessed by a lost love, so I run and see you in a shadow,
the lost and lonely kind.
Just a mirage, an image, chasing me around,
how do you leave a lost love behind?
The love you stole back from me has got me out of control;
you've got to know it's true. I love you, heart and soul.
The love I hold for you is so deep, it knows no fear of depth,
and it just keeps getting stronger.
The love I have for you is rare as an ocean at a standstill, and I
can't hold back no longer.
I run, for miles, miles, miles, then I see you in a shadow,
the lost and lonely kind.
Or is that my shadow and you are only in my mind?
I'm possessed by a lost love, probably never to be found again,
but that is now my destiny, to hold you in my arms again.

Times of You

07/1982

Days are empty, nights are long, sorrow taunts my mind;
rainbows, friends, a lover are things I just can't find.
In this world, I am alone; no one to share the things I see.
By myself, I dwell upon my best memory.
Times of you gather 'round; it's like living in the past.
I remember how you loved me so, why then, didn't it last?

I Wonder

06/1982

I wonder if maybe you lie awake at night and think of me.
I wonder if maybe you wish I was there,
loving you the way I did before.
I wonder if maybe you still care;
Do you wonder if I'm thinking of you, or
if I want to be by your side having you love me
the way that you used to?
I wonder if your feelings have died.

Waves

09/1982

The white-capped waves rolled into shore; the rain was falling down.
The coastguard was whistling a horn, and you were nowhere around.
I walked to get a closer look, but through the fog, I couldn't see.
It made me think of you and all you meant to me.
I sat in the car, dripping wet, and wondered why you love me no more;
I cried to the song on the radio as I watched the waves rush in to shore.

Too Long

07/1982

Too long without your touch, the feeling so sincere;
too long without your love, I need to have you here.
I dream only of the day I can reach out and touch you,
caress your hands, your face, your skin, the way I used to do.
I'm living for the moment passion blinds both you and I;
we will run to find each other, then we'll both break down and cry.
We'll cry because we're together again; we'll cry for wasted time.
I dream only of the day I am yours, and you are mine.

Blinded

08/1982

So blinded by desire that I just couldn't see
you didn't care for what you once loved; you no longer wanted me.
But it's alright—I'll be just fine. I'm starting over new.
I've thrown away all that is old; now, there is no room for you.
I have no time to be hurt again; I have no need to cry.
I've washed my hands of sorrow; this is my last goodbye.
So blinded by the passion, how could I have known
your only desire was to be free and on your own?
But it's alright; I am okay. I've started over again.
I've let go of the past and put that chapter to an end.
Now, I have no time to feel the pain. There is no need to cry.
I've washed my hands of sorrow, and this is my final goodbye.

Too Late

08/1982

Someday, the passion that has built up inside of you is going to break loose
and grab you from behind.
But too late, whether or not you have yours, I'll be here with mine.
There is no going back to get what we had before; the past is gone for good.
And too late, you'll realize, you just didn't try as well as you could.
Someday, you, too, will regret the way we had to end; you never even said goodbye.
But too late, you didn't even have the courage to watch these eyes of mine cry.
There is no going back to recapture any love that was left behind; your hunger
will go unfed.
But too late, much too late, it's over and done, all has been said.

Free?

09/1982

There you are, totally captivated by your freedom,
the place you chose to dwell.
Alone, now and forever, free is a lot like hell.
Here I am, completely empty, so lost and alone.
Now and forever, sorrow is all I own.
Here we are, miles away from each other,
pride keeping us apart.
Alone, now and forever, breaking each other's heart.

Once

11/1982

I know he loved me once; I know he really cared.
It was in the way he touched me; it was in the love we shared.
I know he truly wanted me, sensuous, simple desire.
It was in the way he held me; I felt the sparks turn to fire.
I know he doesn't love me now; I know he doesn't care anymore/
I heard him saying goodbye before he slammed the door.

Remember When?

08/1983

The days that lie ahead of me
will be emptier now, I'm sure;
I'm left with something that once was love.
Time, now, is the only cure.
Gently as desire, softer than a candle's flame,
you called me love; you whispered my name.
You'd hold me so very close;
kissed me till all passion rose.
We fit together as natural as the ocean and land.
What we had was simple, yet we didn't understand.
Now, here we are, just time away,
killing each other; the pain is hard to bear.
My feelings are being trampled on,
the ones we used to share.
The days that lie ahead of me
will be emptier for a while.
I'm left with something that once was love,
but in time, I'll learn how to once again smile.

Still

09/1982

You have ripped me apart, and you have made me cry.
You've brought me down so far, I thought that I would die.
When the hurt got hard to bear, and I just couldn't take no more,
I'd dream my way through the night and end up on a quiet shore.
I'd lie there naked in the sand, and let the sunshine warm me through,
I want to feel that warmth again; I'd like to be with you.
You've torn me all to pieces and left me longing for your touch,
and even though you're killing me, still, I love you very much.

Hold Me

10/1982

You're going now, you're saying goodbye;
you won't stay to see me cry.
You're leaving now on your own,
on your way to life alone.
You opened the door then turned real slow;
I never wanted for you to go.
Just hold me now while I say goodbye.
Just hold me now, while I die.

I Am Night

11/1982

Winter is as cold as I am; I am night but never dawn.

I thought I was yours forever, but tomorrow, you'll be gone.

We were lovers once, it seems so long ago.

Now, I'm like a river that will no longer flow.

We belonged together once like the stars and the sky.

Now, I'm like the desert, all empty and dry.

November skies are just like me; I am night but never dawn.

I thought you truly loved me, but tomorrow, you'll be gone.

Do Dreams Always Die?
01/1983

The snow was falling down around me,
it all looked so pure, so white,
and I dream it will keep forever
while I'm all alone tonight.
I used to dream we were forever, too,
but then you said goodbye.
Now, while I'm all alone,
I wonder, do dreams always die?

He Knew
12/1982

He knew about love and how it could grow,
and he knew how to end it; just let it go.
He knew how to hold me, just close enough,
and he knew how to hurt me and make my path rough.
He knew how to kiss me, caress me, and care,
and he knew how to kill me, with love I thought was rare.
He knew about passion, sensuous, and true;
he also knew sadness and apathy, too.
He knew about sorrow and how hard I could cry,
and he knew how to leave; he just said goodbye.

Love, It Only Lasts a While

01/1983

I was running, trying to get away from the past; the memories were
right behind me and catching up fast.
I never had a minute I could call my own, always dreaming of you
and the love I had known.
I wanted life to be that way again, as happy as we were before,
but then you had to tell me, you didn't love me anymore.
I stopped to catch my breath and take a look around,
and I knew I was going to like the new things I have found.
I don't miss you anymore; I've forgotten your face, your smile.
Now, I know it's true: Love only lasts a while.

Slowly Dying
01/1983

I watched other people live while I was slowly dying,
and when I was giving up, I watched others who were trying.
You took back the love you gave to me; I cried till all my tears were gone.
Now, everything I have lost, someone else has won.
I'd see other people happy, but my face knows no smile,
and when I'd hear a love song, I'd be sad for a while.
When everyone else was laughing, again, you'd find me crying,
and while the whole world was living, I was slowly dying.

Gone

12/1982

I was running after you; everyone has dreams to chase,
but I wasn't fast enough. Now, you're gone without a trace.
I'm here alone, totally captivated by an everlasting fantasy
that you're the one who will control my very destiny.
I see you, although you're not really here.
You're a knight dressed in armor; you know no depth of fear.
You're the stallion that just jumped from the merry-go-round;
I'm lost within these dreams, just waiting to be found.
I've been running after you; we all have dreams to chase.
But I wasn't fast enough, now you're gone without a trace.

The Gypsy

01/1983

The shattered pieces are coming together;
they are fitting precisely into place,
just as the gypsy told me
as we were sitting face to face.
She said that you'd be here
to fill my nights and days;
the loving would come so natural,
in unpredictable ways.
She told me it was true
that we were meant to be,
to go on together forever
until all eternity.
I dreamed of this happening
and wished it would come true.
I wondered how life would be
hopelessly devoted to you.
Only time will tell now
if the gypsy was sincere;
but this is how she described
how I'd feel when you were near.
The bits and pieces are coming together,
going directly into place,
just as the gypsy told me
as we sat there, face to face.

My Skateboard
08/1978

Right here, I have my skateboard; over there, I see a hill.

I just came from the lawyer; he helped me write a will.

I've done this once before, I got going super fast.

They gave me a speeding ticket… It probably won't be the last.

As I climb to the top of this hill and take one more look around,

I see, now they are taking bets that I will not make it down.

Ready—set—here I go; the speed limit is only thirty.

I see people whizzing by; I must be going fifty.

Down the walkway, across the beach, flying down the pier…

I'm going much too fast to look around; I hope my way is clear.

Now, I've landed in the water; I think I see a whale.

Before he gets me, just one more thing, my skateboard is up for sale.

You
07/1980

I laugh at myself and other people, too,
then I turn crazy when I think of you.
You make me wild, dizzy, insane;
I sit in my chair in the pouring rain.
I jump into a puddle, splash my feet,
let down my hair in the middle of the street.
I run through the park and pick me a flower,
then I wait a while for another rain shower.
I smile at myself; other people, too,
then I go silly when I think of you.
You make me giggle all night long
you make me want to sing a song.
I sing out loud, and people stare;
you're on my mind, so I don't care.
I run through the park, still singing along
till I drop my guitar—can't finish the song.
But it doesn't really matter; I really don't care;
when I get home today, I know you will be there.

My Keepsake
01/1980

Young, pure and innocent, but only in my eyes,
only till I saw you: tall, unique, and wise.
You're my keepsake for tomorrow; you put a song in my heart.
Now, I'm a rainbow chaser, even though we are apart.
Losing you was awful; it caused me so much pain
till I looked a different way and saw what I had gained.
The love in my heart was not put here to stay
because love isn't love until you give it away.
Loving you was beautiful, even though it didn't last;
loving you was special, even though it's in the past.
Now, it's time to move on and grow with each new day,
and now, I can take the time to smell the flowers along the way.

Why Did You Have to Die?

04/1980

You gave me a smile that will never go away;
you put a song in my heart.
Now, every day, I feel like singing, even though we are apart.
You gave me your dreams; now they are mine.
You gave me love; you really cared.
Now, every day is filled with laughter, even though you're not there.
We filled the hours with happiness each day;
we took the bad times along with the good,
then you gave me the children that no one else in this world could.
We had a little baby girl; she was your pride and joy,
and then you said the next one would surely be a boy.
But you had gone before he was born;
you'll never get to see him grow, but country boy,
he is, just like you—I thought you'd want to know.
They are here to fill my days with joy, country boy,
they are just like you. They fill this house with laughter.
I wish that you could be here, too.
Late at night, when this house seems so empty,
when the kids are asleep, sometimes, I cry
because, country boy, I love you so. Why did you have to die?

So In Love

06/1989

I saw you yesterday in town, holding her hand, kissing her face,
whispering softly in her ear, so lost in her embrace.
You came home to me that evening, the way you usually do;
well, maybe I'm a fool, but I'm so in love with you.
You're restless when you're sleeping; I hear you call out her name.
How did your feelings change when mine are still the same?
You're different when you're with me now; your eyes are gray; words are few.
Well, maybe I'm just fatuous, but I'm so in love with you.
What are your intentions now? Do you want me? Do you care?
Are you going to say goodbye now to all we've come to share?
Maybe you don't want me now, since you've found somebody new.
Well, I guess I'm just a fool then, because I am so in love with you.

Dreams for Sale

06/ 1985

Every time I want to see you, you say you haven't got the time;
I think I know what is true; other woman on your mind.
You used to hold me in your arms each night
and spend time with me every day.
What has changed? What is different?
Why have you pushed me so far away?
Now, I have old dreams to sell, but no one wants to buy.
No one needs the pain; no one wants to cry.
I have dreams I want to lose where they never will be found
in a corner far away, they will crush when the walls come tumbling down.
I have memories to get rid of, ones that haunt my mind,
visions so clear, but I don't want to see, wish I could be so blind—
blind to you and what I have had and to you whom I have loved.
Please let me escape this bitterness, I pray to God above.
I have dreams I need to sell, and memories I need to lose;
the only dreams I'll dream again are the ones that I choose.
Does anyone want to buy some dreams that I'm so willing to sell?
Well, let me tell you first: my dreams are made in hell.

Miracles?

07/1986

I don't believe in miracles, because if I did, I'd be with you;
I don't believe in wishes, because my wishes do not come true.
I really don't need a miracle or to wish upon a star,
because I have my dreams, and that is where you are.
I wrapped you up in my fantasy and threw the miracles away;
I took the word "wish" from my dictionary, threw it back into yesterday.
I took all the dreams I've had of you and put them in a hiding place,
and that is where I go. Whenever I need to see your face,
I run into my secret world, get out my dreams, and fantasize once more,
but only for a little while, then I leave and lock the door.
So, I don't need no miracles or wishes to come true,
because whenever I get lonely, I have my dreams of you.

You, Once Again

Every time I start to cry,
it is you who makes me smile;
every time I get ready to go,
it is you who makes me stay a while.
For every day of rain,
there are two days of sun,
and every time I kiss you,
my life has just begun.
Each time I fall to sleep,
I dream you're next to me,
and each time that I awake,
it's you, once again.

I Saw Him Through the Mist

I watched the waves come up to shore, and he was at my side.

I watched the smile upon his face when he came in; it was hard to hide.

I wait for him in my dreams each night soon after I fall to sleep;

I wait for him at my front door, knowing his love is mine to keep.

We love to laugh and sing; we do everything together.

I will be his girl forever; he will be my man.

I will leave him never.

I look into the mist, knowing he'll be there.

I look into the clear, blue sky, knowing our love, we'll always share.

Rainbows

07/1980

For My Daughter

When rainbows fall from the sky to try and make a beautiful day,
someone steals the green and blue, and pushes purple out of the way.
Then it's not a rainbow anymore; it's just a bunch of colors falling down,
but they have no place to land because now no one is around.
Well, I don't care anymore; I have my own rainbow.
She sings me the colors that once were stolen; she follows wherever I go.
When rainbows fall on my windowpane, then very quickly disappear,
it doesn't make me cry no more because my rainbow is always here.
She takes all the colors that ever were and blends them together, so I'll understand
that rainbows aren't so very hard to find, and I love her more than anybody can.

Precious Child

08/1983

My precious child, how much you have grown; now, you're walking to school alone
Precious child, so sweet, so sincere, my heart lights up when you are near.
The times that I share with you make everything worth while,
and when I can't be with you, I carry with me your beautiful, sunny smile.
My precious child who is made with gentle love and care,
when we are together, I see rainbows everywhere.
My precious child, out playing with your friends, I will love you till all eternity ends.

To Angela

02/1980

She has a teddy bear named Moe, and she drinks all her milk;
She is as sweet as apple pie, her skin as soft as silk.
She has imaginary friends; she calls them on the phone to say,
"Won't you come for lunch? I'm all alone today."
She has a bunny and her favorite doll; she taught them how to cook.
When it is time for nap, she reads to them her favorite book.
She can count to ten; she is learning her ABCs;
and when she wants to play a game, she says, "Mommy, come play it with me."
She needs her fishes and rubber ducks when she gets in the bath,
and with her sunny disposition, anyone would want to laugh.
When her gram and grandpa come over, she has so much love to share.
Now, it's time to say goodnight; save me a place—I'll be right there.
Daughter, have sweet dreams tonight; let's say a prayer while I hold your hand.
Then I say, "God, please bless her, because I love her more than anybody can."

Words

02/1980

This paper was empty till I picked up a pen,
and the words that I'm writing cannot be written again.
The mountains are rugged, yet can't be defined;
like under water caves and days far behind.
Love is like a jewel you can never describe,
like the ocean at night or an old Indian tribe.
Stars are like treasures that sparkle in the sky;
words are for writing; words never die.
People are faces that get lost in the crowd;
they all blend together, like hundreds of clouds.
Men are for loving; that's the way it should be.
And if it only happens once, that is enough for me.

Upon A Star

12/2011

The desires we share will take us every place we wish to go;
our paradise is near. Let's hop upon a star and travel far from here.
The passion that I hold for you is far beyond compare;
you're drowning in my love, touch me if you dare.
I cannot find escape from the hold you have on me;
you're everything I've dreamed. Don't ever set me free.
Run faster now, I'm waiting; there is a rainbow falling our way.
Jump on with me if you dare, on to sunnier days.

He Called Me Love

12/1980

Night opened its eyes and borned a whole new day;
I anxiously ran in, just hoping that it would stay,
but time wasn't on my side, and soon the sunlight faded.
The dark crept in again, the night I so much hated.
I sat alone, deep in thought, just waiting for the sun to rise.
When the dawn finally came, it brought tears to my eyes.
Now yesterday is gone forever; so are the kisses and hugs
you once gave me. The only way they can return
is inside my memory.
Yesterday may be all gone, yet
I'll always remember the way it was,
because that was the first time you ever called me *"Love."*

My Pen Is Out Of Ink

04/1980

How many times do I have to write it?
How many times do I have to say?
How many times do you have to look at me
to see I love you in a beautiful way?
I'm running out of words;
my mind is blocked with loving thoughts
My pen is out of ink, and no more can be bought.
So, in these words I have written, you'll have to understand,
my feelings are very real; I love you more than anyone else can.
How many hints do I have to drop?
How far out do I have to go?
How much longer should I hang around
for you to see I love you so?
I'm running out of gas; the roads are getting old.
The trees are wearing thin; the breeze is turning cold.
So, in these words I have written, it will have to be enough
for you to understand that loving you is tough.
How much longer do I have to run to catch up to you?
How much longer will it take for me to get my message through?
I'm running out of words; I'm running out of time.
I'm running out of ways to get you to be mine.
So, in all these words I have written here,
you'll just have to understand
that no matter where you are or where you go,
I will love you more than anyone else can.

I'm A Diamond

07/1978

Listen to me, until all my words are spoke:
I'm a diamond, and diamonds can't be broke.
No matter what you do, I'll never come apart—
beautiful like a diamond, like a piece of art.
Leave me now; I don't care. You were mine for a while.
You filled the dream that I was dreaming,
and I really liked your style.
Do what you've been doing; hurt me. I'll never cry
Remember, I'm a diamond, and diamonds never die.
Listen to me, my words are very clever;
I'm a diamond, and diamonds are forever.

When You Said Goodbye
07/1978

When I can find no peace within myself, sometimes I start to cry;
when the happiness is lost between us, I often wonder why.
We used to have so much to share at the end of every day,
hopes and dreams would carry us through when it was that way.
Today is done, and I sit by the window, looking at the stars above,
wondering if someone will come along whom I can really love.
After a while, I fall asleep and let my dreams take over;
the two of us running wild, through fields of four-leaf clover.
We run endlessly through a meadow that leads us into nowhere,
then suddenly. I awake because I thought I felt you laying there.
But my bed is empty except for me; I begin to cry,
because all I can think about is that you said goodbye.

Fantasy

10/1979

I don't care if you leave me now; you were mine for a while.
You filled the dreams that I'd been having, I really liked your style.
If you leave me now, I do not care; I knew this dream had to end.
I can still have my fantasies that you are with me here again.
I live in a world of make believe, where I can be wild and free;
I have my Ferris wheel made from clouds that overlooks the sea.
Whenever I need to get away, up with the birds, I fly.
I follow an eagle over the rainbow, where I let my tears run dry.
I live in a world of make believe, where all my fantasies seem real.
I can be a rose, a thorn, a butterfly; I can be whatever I feel.
So, I don't care if you leave me now; you were mine for a while.
You filled the dreams that I'd been having, and I really liked your style.

I'm Leaving
09/1979

I'm leaving now, I've said goodbye;
don't turn around, don't make me cry.
I've found someone else; I've found somebody new,
and he loves me as much as I once loved you.
You knew it had to be like this; you knew I was going away,
so please don't even think that I'll be back again one day.
I know we had good times together, and that I will never forget.
I'll remember how you once looked at me, the day that we first met.
I do not believe that love is forever; these feelings had to end,
so please don't even think I might be back this way again.
After I am gone, think back to the things we used to do,
then you'll see that no one else can have the part of me I gave to you.
I am ready to leave now; I have said goodbye,
so please don't turn around, please don't make me cry.

Love Is Like...

08/1981

Love: It's like something that has no end;
it's like a desert with no design;
it's like a song that has no melody;
it's a word I cannot define.
Love, it's so confusing,
something I cannot explain.
It's trust and joy and honesty,
yet it is also sorrow and pain.
It's caring and giving and taking;
it's good times along with the bad;
it's kissing and talking and laughing;
it is happy, yet it can also be so sad.
It's like something I cannot describe,
or something that was never there;
it's like something that got lost
and can't be found anywhere.
Love is so confusing;
it leaves no peace of mind,
and maybe love is something
that I will never find.

The Lily Pond Part 77

01/1982

Now, I have to find somewhere else to go,
another place to dump my troubles and hide away the sorrow.
My lily pond is no longer there; the weeping willow is crying, too.
They took away the simple beauty to put up something new.
I've poured my heart out in that lily pond,
whispered secrets I could not keep;
I'd tell all of my darkest thoughts and a love that ran so deep.
There has to be another place as peaceful and gentle somewhere;
I need a place to let my troubles go, and the lily pond is no longer there.